SAGE was founded in 1965 by Sara Miller McCune to support the dissemination of usable knowledge by publishing innovative and high-quality research and teaching content. Today, we publish over 900 journals, including those of more than 400 learned societies, more than 800 new books per year, and a growing range of library products including archives, data, case studies, apps, and video. SAGE remains majority-owned by our founder, and after Sara's lifetime will become owned by a charitable trust that secures our continued independence.

Los Angeles | London | New Delhi | Singapore | Washington DC | Melbourne

ADVANCE PRAISE

Charu's book *#YOU: Build Your Personal Brand* not only articulates the otherwise nebulous concept of a personal brand in clear terms, but it also provides tools for evaluating and improving it. I am sure her readers will find the book very interesting and useful.

S. K. Mohanty, *Whole Time Member,*
Securities and Exchange Board of India and
Director, National Institute of Securities Markets

This book is a one-stop shop to build the greatest asset we have—ourselves. Who does not want to build one's own repute—only if we knew how to do it in a safe manner. Charu explains it all in her highly readable book, presenting the framework for building a powerful personal brand throughout one's career and life.

Robin Banerjee, *Author and Managing Director,*
Caprihans India Limited

Charu is a trainer and a coach with a strong track record of enabling professional success. In an increasingly digital world that is more connected and even more cluttered, it is increasingly important to build a brand that truly defines who we are and what we can deliver. While most of us focus on technical and soft skills, Charu points out that we need to do more for creating awareness of our competencies, areas of interest, accomplishments, and contributions. I am sure professionals across industries will benefit immensely from this book.

Vijay Kumar V., *MD and CEO, National Commodity*
and Derivatives Exchange

This insightful action guide lays down a practical approach to maximize one's value to self and organization. Simple, and lucid, it provides an easy-to-follow plan. I recommend taking the best advantage of this action guide.

V. Kumaraswamy, *Author,*
Columnist and CFO, JK Paper Ltd

The book presents four important aspects of a personal brand—domain knowledge, networking, visibility and presentability. It explains the importance of understanding the political dynamics of an organization and leveraging the social media to enhance one's visibility. Replete with references and real-life examples, the book is a must-read for professionals and start-up entrepreneurs.

Anil Parab, *Executive Vice President and Head,*
L&T Heavy Engineering

Charu has this unique ability to present seemingly impossible soft skills concepts into practical manageable steps. This book showcases the skills that Charu herself demonstrates in every interaction.

Anil Bhatt, *EVP and Regional Director,*
SBI Life Insurance Co. Ltd

If you want to be widely known for one thing, then please grab this book. Charu has found a simple way to communicate the powerful process of building one's own personal branding. The frameworks and tools are easy to practise. A handy guide for all professionals.

Mohinish Sinha, *Partner, Deloitte*

In the digital world, building your personal brand is more important than ever, and especially so in this post-lockdown, new world of work. Towards that, Charu's book is something that all professionals need to read. What makes the book engaging are the diagrammatic representation of concepts and the exercises for self-improvement. Charu has also employed storytelling which enhances the reader engagement.

Vikram Chaudhary, *Assistant Editor,* The Financial Express

In today's world, building a strong personal brand that stands out from the crowd and defines you has become increasingly important. Charu Sabnavis handholds you through the exercise of systematically building a strong personal brand based on your core strengths and expertise. Using easy to understand graphics, storytelling and exercises, the book is an easy-to-follow guide to personal brand building.

Alokananda Chakraborty, *Formerly with* Business Standard

Charu has found a simple and compelling way to pull together the science and art of personal branding. Comprehensive, focused and immediately useful, the book is an articulate and a highly readable synthesis of the principles of personal branding and a framework for applying these principles in real-life situations. The book is a must-read for current and aspiring leaders.

Atul Srivastava, *Founder CEO, Effective People and Former Head HR, Capgemini India*

The book is very well written and, in a simple way, guides the reader through the building blocks of creating and enhancing the personal brand. I loved the way the storytelling technique has been used by Charu to demonstrate some of the concepts. The action-based approach is commendable as it aims to embed the learning in the reader's psyche.

Mukta Arya, *Regional Head of Human Resources Societe Generale (APAC)*

The 'four dimensions of a personal brand' explained in the book gives the reader a clear direction on things-to-do to build one's brand. The book is supported with stories which enhance the recall value, and the simple, easy-to-use and high-impact tools and exercises deepen one's self-awareness and put the reader on the path of developing and strengthening the personal brand. This is a must-have book in everyone's personal library.

Akshaya Kashyap, *Vice President, Human Resources, Future Generali India Insurance Company Limited*

Besides the fact that Charu's book deep dives into the 'what' of personal brand building, it also comes in at a time when each one of us had had an excruciating pandemic event that has led us to introspect and self-assess even more on building our personal equity and brand. I highly recommend Charu's *#YOU: Build Your Personal Brand*. It is for everyone as it successfully addresses presumably the greatest question never asked by many—what is my personal value proposition and how do I strengthen it? Go ahead, engage with the book and you will emerge a different person.

Abhishek Jha, *Vice President, HR, Writer Information*

#YOU: Build Your Personal Brand provides a refreshing and an integrated approach on personal branding. In this book, Charu has skilfully crafted a narrative and offered a tapestry for young and emerging professionals to introspect, discover and build an impactful and authentic personal brand needed to be successful in our modern society. I would categorize this book as a do-it-yourself guide on personal branding.

Ravi Kingrani, *Head Capability Development, Global Banking and Markets, HSBC*

Every one of us wants to leave an impact, build a network that opens doors and tell our story in a memorable way. But to do that we need help. I believe *#YOU: Build Your Personal Brand* by Charu Sabnavis is just the book to get you started on this journey of learning to pay attention to who you are and how you can leave a positive impression. The book has handy tools, lots of practice opportunities and a clear, thorough structure. No young professional can afford to miss this stepping stone to a better career.

Seema Chowdhry, *Vice President,*
Curriculum Harappa Education

Charu has stepped up to demystify an area that, at best, has got scattered attention—either remaining theoretical or leaning towards tips and tricks. Her book offers both—captivating clarity of the relevant concepts and very practical methods that can be easily learned. I see this as a powerful playbook on the subject. Any corporate executive who believes in the power of building impactful relationships must read this; it *will* make a difference.

Raj Bowen, *Founder and Leadership Coach, New Directions*

I congratulate Ms Charu Sabnavis for this very useful work on personal branding. In a highly competitive world laden with information overload, both youngsters and those in their mid-careers are often directionless on how to prove and present their worth. This book is in fact a manual for those struggling to prove themselves, and I recommend it not only for students on the threshold of employment but also professionals at different stages in their career.

Dr V. R. Narasimhan, *Dean, School of Corporate*
Governance and School of Regulatory Studies

This book fills a vital knowledge gap as most people are unaware of their own shortcomings in one or more of the four dimensions of their personal brand. The book is rich and holistic, with a clear-cut roadmap in a less-explored area.

Professor Sunder Ram Korivi, *Senior Consultant,*
Department of Economic Affairs, National Institute
of Financial Management Research Cell

#You

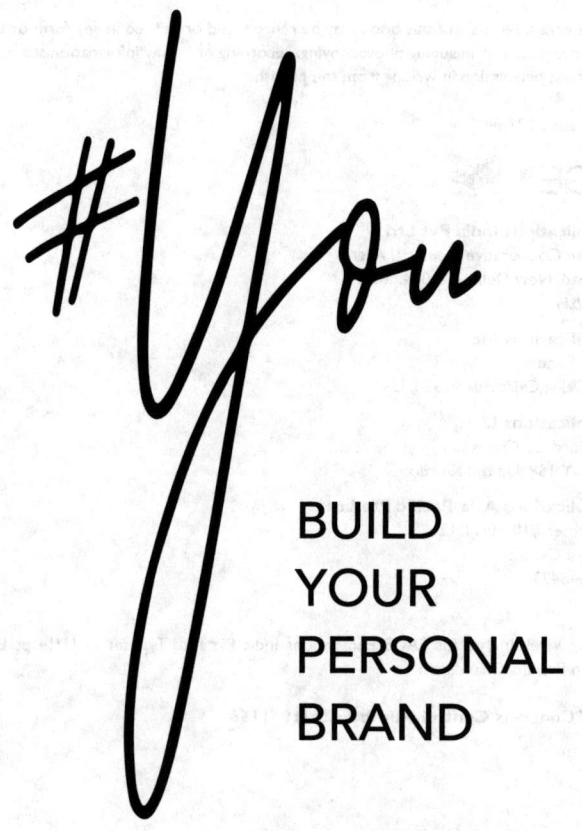

BUILD
YOUR
PERSONAL
BRAND

CHARU SABNAVIS

Los Angeles | London | New Delhi
Singapore | Washington DC | Melbourne

First published in 2021 by

SAGE Publications India Pvt Ltd
B1/I-1 Mohan Cooperative Industrial Area
Mathura Road, New Delhi 110 044, India
www.sagepub.in

SAGE Publications Inc
2455 Teller Road
Thousand Oaks, California 91320, USA

SAGE Publications Ltd
1 Oliver's Yard, 55 City Road
London EC1Y 1SP, United Kingdom

SAGE Publications Asia-Pacific Pte Ltd
18 Cross Street #10-10/11/12
China Square Central
Singapore 048423

Published by Vivek Mehra for SAGE Publications India Pvt Ltd. Typeset in 11/14 pt Baskerville by Fidus Design Pvt Ltd, Chandigarh.

Library of Congress Control Number: 2021941156

ISBN: 978-93-91370-42-8 (PB)

SAGE Team: Neha Pal, Ankit Verma, Shivani Damle and Rajinder Kaur

For my husband, Madan,
who has helped me discover the writer in me,
my daughter Ragini, who has constantly added a unique palette of
music, colour and humour to life, and my parents,
Anil and Manju Jain, who have always supported
my decisions and chosen paths.

Thank you for choosing a SAGE product!
If you have any comment, observation or feedback,
I would like to personally hear from you.

Please write to me at **contactceo@sagepub.in**

Vivek Mehra, Managing Director and CEO, SAGE India.

CONTENTS

This book has been an eye-opener.

I work on building brands for a living yet never thought of consciously building my own brand. The first time I became aware of the possibility of applying brand-building techniques to myself was a year ago—when Charu Sabnavis met me to discuss the concept of this book and to interview me for it.

Her questions prompted me to look at myself as a brand. It is not that I was oblivious to the fact that I had a public persona. I already did some of the things that help build a personal brand: I spoke to the media about my work, for example, as that is a standard part of my job. But I shied away from strategically plugging myself. It seemed akin to bragging—a behaviour one was brought up to eschew. And I certainly did not evaluate myself—objectively—as a brand.

After reading the manuscript of this book, I discovered that there is so much you can do for your brand: At one level, getting your personal branding right is about getting your story right. This book is bursting with stories—original case studies of Indian professionals from every field and every level. You invariably relate to their journeys, their challenges—you see yourself in them and suddenly you become self-aware. You say, 'Hey, I do things like this and it helps me take my career forward.' Or 'I've behaved like that—and now I realize that that particular behaviour held me back professionally.' And the whiff of 'self-promotion' suddenly becomes irrelevant.

The Indian case studies are not the only stories in the book. There are insightful anecdotes about international brand names like Sheryl Sandberg, Thomas L. Friedman and Edward de Bono, instructive stories from Greek mythology and the British monarchy, a telling scene from a Hollywood movie, the unique distribution strategy of a Bollywood blockbuster, the symbolism of characters from a Rudyard Kipling tale and the reinvention of a Van Gogh painting—all coming together to form a rich, resplendent mosaic of transformational personal branding lessons.

Charu Sabnavis coaches you through this book with easy-to-implement tips: How to leverage the power of 3 when telling your story, for example. Or how to apply the research on the power of clothing, and even on what sort of photo works best on social media. Simple yet invaluable tips. And, for the more technically inclined, there are models, tables and toolkits to help you evaluate your brand, identify your strengths and weaknesses and progress with precision to the next level.

Wherever you are in the working world, success means getting your own story right, and telling your own story right.

This is the 'how to' manual that will get you there.

Sumanto Chattopadhyay,
Chairman and Chief Creative Officer
82.5 Communications, Ogilvy Group

ACKNOWLEDGEMENTS

Frequently running short of ideas as well as words, I remember my struggle with the tedium of essay writing during my formative years. I had never counted writing, even remotely, as one of my strengths. My rendezvous with the written word began when my husband, Madan, who has authored four books and hundreds of articles, pushed, cajoled, persuaded and propelled me to explore writing.

I wrote my first article thinking, 'Who would want to publish this?' Not even in my wildest dreams did I anticipate any publication agreeing to carry it. But I was pleasantly surprised—shocked, flabbergasted—when my maiden article was published on 'The Learning Curve' page in the *Economic Times*. Subsequently I went on to write several articles on leadership, workplace excellence and diversity for some of the leading newspapers. I reached out to a host of people in this context—subject matter experts, practitioners and other stalwarts in their fields—gathering diverse thoughts, ideas, perspectives and stories and incorporating them in the articles. These added immense richness and value to the narratives. I would like to acknowledge the contribution of Yogi Sriram, Raj Bowen, Suchitra Bhaskar, Anil Parab, Chandrashekhar Mukherjee, Akshaya Kashyap, Atul Srivastava, Sunil Warrier, Abhishek Jha and Anil Bhatt in this context.

A very special thanks goes to Vikram Chaudhary, Assistant Editor, the *Financial Express*, Seema Chowdhry, former associate editor, *Mint*, and journalist Alokananda Chakraborty, formerly with *Business Standard*, for providing me a platform that offered visibility, besides helping me hone my writing skills. It is the articles published in these newspapers that triggered my tryst with SAGE, leading to the subsequent opportunity to write this book.

I would like to acknowledge my daughter Ragini, who brainstormed with me on several occasions when I was conceptualizing this book, bringing in her creativity, spontaneity and imagination. I have captured scores of her personal experiences in the book.

I have been fortunate to be able to bounce off ideas with my brother-in-law, Madhukar, and sister-in-law, Farida, on several occasions. They have readily shared an eclectic assortment of compelling anecdotes, episodes and personal experiences from their rich corporate journeys, besides connecting me with people who, in turn, provided more ideas. In fact, Madhukar introduced me to Sumanto Chattopadhyay, who was the first person I had interviewed as a part of my research for this book, and who very graciously, later, agreed to write the foreword for this book.

I am grateful to the people listed below for making time for conversations to share their personal stories and experiences, all of which have enhanced the substance, richness and engagement of the book.

1. Abhijit Bhaduri

2. Alok Jha

3. Amogh Deshmukh

4. Aruna Jonna

5. Arvind Charanyan V.

6. Chandra Sekhar, A. K. N. R.

7. Chetan Walawalkar

8. Chetna Vasishth

9. Harsha Jhunjhunwala

10. Harshaja Ajinkya

11. Jenita Mercy

12. Madhu Khatri

13. Meghana Biwalkar

14. Natasha Bhutani

15. Prasad Ajinkya

16. Purna Chandra Rao Duggirala

17. Rakesh Kumar

18. Shruthi Upadya

19. Sumanto Chattopadhyay

20. Vijayraj Kamat

21. Yogi Sriram

A big thank you also to the below-listed people for endorsing this book. Their endorsement, I am sure, will go a long way in encouraging potential readers to explore the book.

1. Abhishek Jha

2. Akshaya Kashyap

3. Alokananda Chakraborty

4. Anil Bhatt

5. Anil Parab

6. Atul Srivastava

7. Mohinish Sinha

8. Mukta Arya

9. Raj Bowen

10. Ravi Kingrani

11. Robin Banerjee

12. Seema Chowdhry

13. S. K. Mohanty

14. Sunder Korivi

15. V. Kumaraswamy

16. Vijay Kumar V.

17. Vikram Chaudhary

18. V. R. Narasimhan

And last (but certainly not least), I am thankful to Neha Pal of SAGE for helping me curb my proclivity for procrastination, thus ensuring the timely completion of this book. The credit for some of the catchy chapter and topic headings in the book goes entirely to her.

INTRODUCTION

Rahul Mehra was an experienced, result-oriented, collaborative sales manager at a fast-moving consumer goods (FMCG) company manufacturing a variety of toothpastes, managing an important territory in the north zone. He was performing well, achieving his sales targets and managing his clients and team effectively. He was quiet and efficient, got along well with people and was liked by his colleagues.

He had been up for promotion for two years in a row but had consistently missed the cut. While his work was appreciated, he was considered as 'not yet ready' for more senior-level roles. In the current year, for instance, his peer Rajiv, a sales manager from the south zone, was promoted to the coveted zonal head role, much to Rahul's chagrin, who was suitably disappointed, felt let down and was immensely distressed. 'Haven't I given it my 100 per cent, every day, 10 hours a day, weekends and holidays, whatever it took? The system has been so unfair in ignoring my contribution!' he thought bitterly. His first instinct was to march to his manager's cabin and put in his papers.

Why was Rahul passed over despite his success on the assigned tasks? Where did he fall short?

Four Stages of Contribution

Let's map Rahul's career trajectory to the global organizational consulting firm,[1] Korn Ferry's Four Stages of Contribution Model, which is based on the research of former Harvard Business School professors, Dr Gene Dalton and Dr Paul Thompson. The model outlines four well-defined stages in a person's career trajectory

Figure I.1. The Four Stages of Contribution

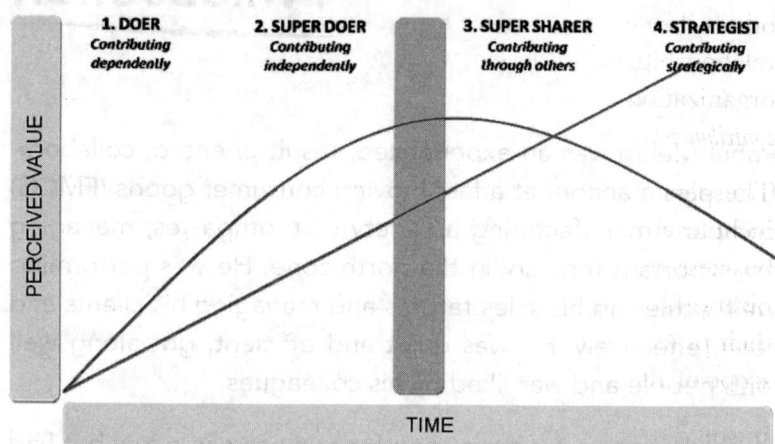

Source: Adapted from 'The Four Stages of Contribution Research' by Korn Ferry. https://www.kornferry.com/content/dam/kornferry/docs/article-migration/Korn-Ferry-Institute-The-Four-Stages.pdf

and establishes a direct correlation between a career stage and their contribution to the organization. It lays down the criteria for success in each stage as well as performance elements that would position a person favourably for the next stage.

A person who has just transitioned from campus to the workplace is considered to be in Stage 1 of their career. They are expected to learn the nuts and bolts of their role, perform routine tasks, seek guidance and work under supervision. A person *contributes dependently* in Stage 1.

As a person enhances their functional competence by inculcating and deepening their technical skills and knowledge, building their credibility as an expert in the field, gaining the confidence of their superiors and taking responsibility for definable projects, they start *contributing independently* and enter Stage 2.

Having excelled as an individual contributor, the person enters Stage 3 as a result of further developing the depth and breadth of technical skills, taking responsibility to manage and mentor others, bringing new ideas to the table, building cross functional relationships and developing the credibility to represent the organization to clients and other external groups. The person now *contributes through others*.

The person enters Stage 4 when their role further broadens to include strategic elements like identifying and driving critical business opportunities, contributing towards growing the organization's leadership pipeline and giving a strategic direction to their practice, vertical, function or the company depending on the scope of their role. They *contribute strategically* in this stage.

It would be worthwhile to note that first, the stages of contribution are not directly tied to particular positions or levels in an organization. Second, the course of a person's career is likely to be nonlinear, marked by curves and loops and ups and downs. Third, a person could be engaged in multiple stages simultaneously. For instance, a project manager could be in stage one with respect to a project that entails learning new age, cutting edge technology. Concurrently, they could be in Stage 3 with respect to another project which they may be running with minimal supervision, having delegated the day-to-day matters to the team.

A pertinent question worthy of reflection is that as a person transitions through their career how should their perceived value in the organization change with time. Logically, the stakeholders should observe a strong growth in the value that the person brings to the table over time. However, it is seen that many a manager, in fact, fumble and struggles. The transition between Stages 2 and 3 is an inflection point, where the perceived value of a person often starts to decline or plateau.

Why is this transition difficult?

It is seen that managers continue to concentrate on tasks that they have excelled in and which have contributed to their success thus far. They continue to engage in Stage 2 type activities with their focus limited to their teams, clients and the assigned projects. They view the ability to deliver the project within the projected time and cost as the yardstick for excellence and success, little realizing that with each successive career stage, they are progressively operating on a larger turf in terms of both the complexity of the assigned tasks, as well as the intricacies of the relationships that they need to manage with an increasingly larger number of stakeholders. This calls for enhancing their impact and influence and changing their perspective from narrow to broad, short term to long term and from technical to strategic and relational. They need to exhibit elements of Stage 3 and 4 type activities and behaviours such as developing business acumen, discerning opportunities and threats, dealing with ambiguity, grooming talent and building a leadership pipeline, questioning the status quo and bringing about efficiencies, developing a robust internal and external network, and building the credibility for being able to present the organization in various internal and external forums. This calls for developing new mindsets, inculcating new skills and engaging in new activities, which a number of managers don't realize; which is why their career graph tends to hit a plateau.

And this is perhaps where Rahul Mehra (mentioned at the beginning of the Introduction) was struggling. Caught in a treadmill between stages 2 and 3, he was unable to inculcate the skills and the minset needed to transition effectively to stage 4. Yogi Sriram, Advisor, Group HR, Larsen & Toubro, says,

In order for someone to remain relevant and continue to be perceived as adding value, it is imperative for him/her to remain a life-long learner, in terms of sharpening and enhancing the domain knowledge, taking the initiative to inculcate skills pertinent for the current, and even more importantly, the next role, like the ability to influence stakeholders, communicate with impact and precision

and make decisions in an environment of ambiguity.
Very often, people tend to settle into their zones of
comfort, sink into complacency, become risk averse and
resist treading unchartered territory. As a result not only
does their learning take a hit, their perceived value also
starts to rust and wane. For instance, in today's context,
saying I am not tech savvy is concomitant to saying I am
not literate.

A case in point is a Silicon Valley chief executive officer (CEO),[1] one of the pioneers of the technology around flash memory, a *memory* chip used in digital cameras, computers, MP3 players and smart phones. He frequently features on CNBC shows and has been delivering business presentations for over 20 years. Carmine Gallo, the author of *Five Stars: The Communication Secrets to Get from Good to Great*, recounts a meeting with him in a *Harvard Business Review* article, as this CEO had approached him for—hold your breath—an engagement to help him sharpen his public speaking skills! To Gallo's question as to why he felt he needed to improve, considering his success and excellence as an orator, he responded, 'I can always get better. Every point up or down in our share price means billions of dollars in our company's valuation. How well I communicate makes a big difference.'

This, to my mind, is a manifestation of what life-long learning means. Amogh Deshmukh, Managing Director, Development Dimensions International, India, an international human resources (HR) and leadership development consultancy, remarks,

People tend to hit a flat terrain in their career trajectory
for many reasons—failure to constantly learn and rein-
vent themselves in a dynamic environment, inability to
navigate through the organization's political fabric, inept-
ness in engaging with a strong executive presence, or
simply falling short in their intellectual capability.

These are some of the nuanced expectations of an organization which may neither be stated explicitly in the job description, nor show up in the key result areas identified for a role. These are, however, critical in increasing one's impact and influence, staying valuable in one's current role and positioning oneself favourably for the next. In fact, many managers are unable to make the behavioural change and the psychological shift that are required for a successful transition.

This book presents a framework for building a powerful personal brand incorporating skills, behaviours and perspectives that enable people to drive their careers and transitions between different career stages successfully.

Reference

1. Gallo C. What it takes to give a great presentation. Harv Bus Rev [Internet]. 6 Jan 2020. Available from: https://hbr.org/2020/01/what-it-takes-to-give-a-great-presentation

01

Defining
a Brand

Chapter 1

What Is a Personal Brand?

Start with an organization. What words come to your mind when you think of brand Tata? The immediate responses I have heard from hundreds of people to whom I have posed this question are—reliable, conglomerate, multinational, humungous, socially responsible and employee friendly, among others. How about Apple? What do you associate Apple with? *Innovative, expensive, high-end, best in class and multinational* are some of the adjectives that people have frequently expressed. Have you noticed how the adjectives associated with Tata are very distinct from those related with Apple? People obviously perceive Tata very differently from how they see Apple.

What has triggered these impressions? People have gathered impressions from their direct experience with Tata or Apple as employees, customers, suppliers, business partners, bankers or regulators. Their perceptions are also shaped indirectly by what they hear from family, friends and neighbours or read in the press or on the social media. The sum total of all these impressions either lends itself to enhance the brand equity or to mitigate it. Two points emerge from this—first, the perception of people is crucial in shaping a brand, and second, the brand itself is a dynamic entity, constantly adjusting to people's perception based on their direct and indirect experiences.

What holds for an organization applies just as much to people. Every time people interact individually or in groups, socially at the water cooler and lunch tables, or professionally at meetings and conferences, they form impressions about each other. These impressions emanate from how a person comes across in term of communication style, collaboration, creativity, technical and problem-solving skills, punctuality, adherence to timelines, ability to pitch an idea or address a difficult interpersonal situation effectively. Needless to say, these impressions can either be positive or negative. The collage that emerges as a result of clubbing all these impressions represents the brand of a person.

A brand is really one's identity or the reputation that one enjoys amongst one's stakeholders. Jeff Bezos, the founder and CEO of Amazon, had famously said, 'Your brand is what other people say about you when you're not in the room.'

Chairman and chief creative officer of 82.5 Communications, Ogilvy Group, India, Sumanto Chattopadhyay said,

A brand is the way you come across to the world. It cuts across your outmost layer comprising the visual and the audio, the way you appear and sound, to your core, encompassing your personal values and what you stand for. I am known for being outspoken, whether in a personal, an internal organizational or a client setting, and transparent, to the point of being blunt. I think of this as a strength and it is deeply embedded in my brand, but, of course, it has also landed me into trouble on several occasions, and with age and experience, therefore, I have learnt to temper it down and engage with greater discretion.

Clearly, perceptions of people, since they feed into a brand, are important. In the marketplace, perception is reality. A brand, therefore, is dynamic, constantly evolving as a result of how your stakeholders experience you in different situations.

Define Your Brand

What is the hallmark of your brand? How would you define it? What do you want to be known for? Answering these questions is a crucial starting point in designing and building a brand that enables, facilitates and assists in giving your career a forward thrust.

Prannoy Roy, for instance, is known for digital journalism, anchoring popular TV shows featuring the budget, election analysis and other news elements. What may not be widely known is that he is also an author, a chartered accountant and an economist.

Whom do you associate the term 'lateral thinking' with? Edward de Bono, of course! He is an authority in the field of creative thinking, teaching of thinking as a skill and author of over 60 books on the subject. What is less widely known about him is that he has two degrees in medicine from the University of Malta and Trinity College.

And who comes to mind when you think of stock market investments? None other than Rakesh Jhunjhunwala, a chartered accountant by qualification, known for his acumen of stock market investment and dubbed as the Oracle of Dalal Street.

Simon D'Souza, an HR professional at a global investment bank, was friendly and helpful with a pleasant demeanour. Having a knack for making friends easily, he was known for his relationship building and networking skills. He had a pulse of the environment in terms of who was in favour and who was not, who was active in the job market and who was slated for a new role, by virtue of being a part of several formal and informal groups, both within and outside the organization. I remember the time we were contemplating a firm-wide learning festival as a forum to engage employees in some serious, technical, along with some lighter, fun-packed learning interventions. We did not have to look far and wide for speakers, instructors and trainers as Simon knew a yoga teacher, a Zumba instructor, a foxtrot trainer as well as a scuba diving instructor, all of whom were willing to collaborate pro bono, because of his personal connect, to make this zero-budget event a roaring success. Simon was also known for his meticulousness and attention to detail. In fact, he had been awarded a prize for managing the very complex logistics for the organization's campus recruitment drive impeccably.

Ashwini Nath, a digital marketing executive in an e-commerce company, was recognized for going the extra mile, being completely invested in ensuring successful product launches and being available 24x7. She says,

I had to work with cross functional teams, without the positional power to really flip things around. So, I invested time in building relationships and devised a very efficient tracking system. I would identify the to-dos for the day and diligently touch base with everyone in the team to see if things were on track. On perceiving a potential problem that was beyond my scope of control, I was quick to escalate matters to my seniors, never hesitating to call them at late hours, and connect the relevant stakeholders to seek a resolution.

Bharat Singh, known for his writing skills, became the go-to person for any writing assignments for the department like documenting articles on employee engagement events and successful project completions and posting them on the firm's internal social media platform. He was often called upon to whet any important email messages that were slated to go out on behalf of the department.

While each of these people would certainly have expertise in multiple domains which would have contributed to the overall power of their brand, the brand itself is defined around a single overpowering element.

For a brand to stand out, it needs to be crisp and well defined. Nebulousness takes the edge off a brand. Indra Nooyi, the former CEO of PepsiCo, made this point in her keynote address at BlogHer, a cross-platform media network and publisher for women, in 2011, when she said, 'Leaders need to have a hip pocket skill that everybody looks at and says that XYZ is the go-to person for that skill. Because unless you are really known for something and not just as a generalist, you don't stand out from the pack.'[1]

Adjust Your Brand

Simon was naturally meticulous and a people's person and hence his brand came to be associated with these attributes; Ashwini was excellent at execution as she had it in her to give her 100 per cent to whatever she did and Bharat had a talent for writing. These were their inherent qualities which defined their brand. But this happened more by chance than by design. It was not a conscious outcome.

A powerful brand, however, does not evolve by chance or by accident. It is a managed outcome. It has to be carefully and strategically cultivated through a calculated set of actions, in the context of a goal.

It is a huge advantage for Simon to be known for his networking skills, but if he is an aspiring soft skills trainer, he needs to look for opportunities to hone his training delivery skills to create a more well-rounded identity for himself and take the requisite steps to draw the attention of his stakeholders to this identity. Similarly, if Ashwini is seeking to be a marketing professional, being stellar at execution is a huge advantage, but she needs to reshape her identity in view of this goal. She may now want to grow her identify beyond execution to excellence in client interactions. She needs to actively seek assignments, take initiatives and work on projects that would strengthen her desired identity and reshape her professional reputation.

Chetna Vasishth demonstrates this by rebranding and reinventing herself successfully over three career shifts that she has undertaken.

As an ambitious young woman, Vasishth embarked upon a banking career soon after completing her MBA and spent the next 10 years driving sales and business development at multinational banks like ANZ Grindlays Bank and Standard Chartered. She then decided to opt out of a very rewarding and promising career in the banking industry, in favour of teaching courses in marketing at leading business schools like the Indian Institute of Management at Bangalore and the Indian Institute of Planning and Management at Mumbai in the capacity of visiting faculty. 'Teaching students was a completely different ball game. The experience helped me hone my subject knowledge as well as my teaching skills, besides allowing me to devote more quality time towards my family,' she said.

Five years into teaching, Vasishth was already contemplating her next move. She decided to blend her knowledge of the banking domain with her teaching experience to start a training and development consulting firm, Learning Tree, in 2007. She ran successful training programs in banking operations and key account management programs for a corporate audience this time, engaging with leading banks such as HDFC Bank, Kotak Mahindra Bank, IDBI bank, Société Générale and Deutsche Bank, amongst others.

Eight years into corporate training, as disenchantment with the corporate learners and their sense of entitlement set in, Vasishth got restless yet again and started to explore opportunities elsewhere. Around that time, she was invited for a panel discussion on the future of careers at a management institute. As the discussion progressed, she sensed that the educators perhaps had a total disconnect with the audience—the students. The students were, in fact, being preached rather than have their real problems and needs addressed. A lot of students, she realized, dreamt about pursuing foreign degrees but had no clue about how to proceed. The students and their parents were really looking for guidance around available career options, degrees that would get them there, the application process and ways to muster finance. The available counselling was not only expensive but emanated from vested interests in recommending colleges that gave higher commissions. This realization triggered Vasishth's next career move. She had got her calling in providing authentic career guidance to the youth. She sought to do this through a chat show. ChetChat, which is one of India's top online chat shows in the career and education space today, was thus born. The show has featured over 200 videos with more than 5 million views and 1 million subscribers since its launch in 2015.

How did she rebrand and reinvent herself multiple times? What did it entail? Vasishth says,

Every time I have made a career shift I have started from ground zero. Totally displaced from my comfort zone, I have been called upon to operate on a completely new turf and pick up and master brand new skills. When I started ChetChat, for instance, I knew nothing about social media or what went into creating a video. I set off on a very steep learning curve by initially attending videography and video editing workshops at the YouTube Space at the Film City in Mumbai.

There are certain inflection points in one's career that emanate either from an intended career shift, as in Vasishth's case, or from an organic career progression, as explained in the Four Stages of Contribution model in the chapter Introduction, to sail through which one needs to inculcate new skills and behaviours. A concomitantly evolving brand that demonstrates these skills and behaviours can render these transitions smooth and seamless.

Personal branding, therefore, is a process where you establish, readjust and constantly reinforce who you are and what you stand for, in terms of your knowledge, skills and values, to address your current and future goals. It requires constant monitoring, frequent reality checks and repeated reinforcement. Needless to say, this entails a great deal of hard work and self-discipline. Yogi Sriram, Advisor, Group HR, Larsen & Toubro says, 'Brands don't last forever and brand building, therefore, needs to be a continuous process. It is important to redefine and rediscover your personal brand periodically, adding skills and capabilities along the way for it to remain relevant and current.'

Add a Side Hustle

'Passionate pursuits and extra-curricular interests outside your primary domain enhance the appeal and charisma of a brand,' says Sriram.

For instance, Sriram is passionate about trains and has a collection of over 62 trains of different forms, shapes and sounds—some with whistles, others with bells and horns and yet others with a chuff or a baritone diesel sound. He even has railway tracks on the ceiling of his living room. 'It is my passion to learn and practice electronics and I do the electronics in my digital trains myself,' he says. He is also passionate about photography and has done a stunning photoshoot of flamingos off the coast of Sewri, on the eastern edge of South Mumbai, in Maharashtra in February 2020, with his brand new Nikon 500 mm prime lens.

Similarly, in addition to being an advertising professional par excellence, Chattopadhyay is an amateur photographer, an actor and a passionate English language enthusiast. His varied interests have culminated in a series of engaging, humorous and educative videos on the English language, titled 'The English Nut'. These videos, posted on the social media, highlight several interesting aspects of the language like the etymology and pronunciation of words, palindromes—words that read the same forward and backward, and anagrams—words formed by rearranging letters of other words and the like. This side hustle has allowed him to broaden his brand to a multifarious, well rounded one.

An ardent cricket fan, Madan Sabnavis, an economist by profession, engages in conversations around cricket with as much fervour, enthusiasm and comprehension as when he is discussing the different facets of the economy. Armed with an elephant's memory for cricket statistics, he talks excitedly about Clive Lloyd's match winning 102 off 85 balls in the 1975 West Indies–Australia World Cup final and the carnage wreaked by Vivian Richards and Collis King on the English bowers, including Richards's iconic six off the last ball, which helped West Indies clinch the World Cup in the 1979 finals against England. His all-time favourite cricketer? The indestructible, arrogant, gum chewing, 'helmet-less', confident King Richards, of course!

Similarly, I met a business analyst during one of my training programs at a global accounting firm who said that he enjoys solo travel and had travelled to 47 countries! Another participant in the same program was passionate about cars. He made time to travel around the country, on top of a very hectic job, having attended most of the major automobile shows in India. And, of course, there are others who run marathons, tender to their gardens, paint, sketch, trek and climb.

Brands built purely around professional and domain expertise, while certainly powerful, tend to get boring. Side hustles, by adding an element excitement, add vibrancy to a brand.

Perform a Reality Check

My manager had once offered me feedback to the effect that my direct reports perceived me as unapproachable. This had come to me as a revelation as I had always considered myself friendly, approachable and easy going. Psychologists have coined the term 'transparency illusion' to represent this feeling where we think that people see us the way we think we are. In reality, of course, there could be a divergence.

The feedback led me to reflect on my team interactions, my reactions, behaviour and body language that I was possibility displaying which had triggered this perception. As a result of this introspection, I started engaging with my team with greater awareness towards my reactions, expressions and body language and consciously adjusting my style and approach in a bid to change this perception.

It would be judicious, therefore, to gauge the conscious or unconscious impact that you have on people as these perceptions feed into your brand and are, therefore, important in determining the extent of your influence as well as your career trajectory in terms of chances for promotion, prospects for that coveted role or the career-enhancing assignment that you are seeking.

Your brand centres around the unique combination of your strengths, weaknesses, drivers, skills, knowledge and passions that you embody, and the values and fundamental principles that you stand for. The unique value proposition that your brand represents helps people make decisions about whether they should hire you, promote you, assign you, do business with you or be your friend. Your quest to strengthen your brand and reorient it in a way so that people make these decisions in your favour, thereby promoting your career and supporting the accomplishment of your goals, must start with a brand audit. A brand audit comprises the following steps.

1. Introspect on the key elements of your brand.

2. Understand how your stakeholders perceive you.

3. Identify gaps between your self-perception and the way you are perceived by others.

4. Design a plan to bridge gaps, if any.

5. Identify elements that you need to add to your brand in the context of your goals and your next career move.

Follow these steps to carry out your personal brand audit. We will revisit this exercise at the end of the book to help you think through these questions again and fine tune or re-design your action plan for strengthening your brand based on the ideas presented in the book that resonate with you.

1. Introspection

Think through the following points and document them in Table 1.1.

- Identify your top five strengths.
- Identify your top five developmental areas.
- Identify your values.
- Identify your passions and interests.
- What sets you apart from your peers?

2. Validation

- Identify five people with whom you have interacted in different work situations, who know you well and are likely

Table 1.1: How Am I Perceived?

Parameter	Self	Team	Manager	Client
Strengths				
Developmental areas				
Values				
Passions				

to offer candid feedback. These could be your manager, clients, peers or direct reports.

- Ask them the following questions and document them in Table 1.1.

  o How do you perceive me?

  o Name five areas of strength and five areas of improvement that you have noticed.

  o What can I do differently to be more successful?

- Manage your reactions appropriately and resist the temptation to explain, defend or express disappointment. Ask for examples or clarification, if required.

- Thank the person sincerely for the feedback.

3. Reflection

- Analyse the data you have captured in Table 1.1 by reflecting on the following questions.

  o What are the common themes that are emerging?

  o Is there any deviation between your self-perception and the way others perceive you?

    i.   Are there any strengths that you believe you have which others have not noticed? *Think about ways to display these strengths such that your stakeholders notice them.*

    ii.   Are there any developmental areas that your stakeholders have pointed you to, that you were not aware? *How will you act on this feedback?*

4. Adjustment

- What are your goals for the next two years?

- What skills, knowledge and behaviours do you need to inculcate so as to position yourself well for meeting these goals?

- What actions do you need to take in order that your brand manifests these skills, knowledge and behaviours? How will you demonstrate these?

5. Your Action Plan

- Your brand is your identity or the reputation that you enjoy in the minds of your stakeholders.

- It is the manifestation of your strengths and weakness, knowledge and skills, passions and drivers and, most importantly, the fundamental principles that you stand by. It represents your unique value proposition.

- Your brand is not just about who you are but equally about how the world perceives you. It is important to identify and address the gaps between your self-perception and others' perception of you.

- Your brand needs to be evaluated, adjusted and reoriented periodically in the face of your changing needs so that it serves you well in driving your career and accomplishing your goals.

Reference

1.   PepsiCo. 5Cs of leadership with Indra Nooyi. YouTube. Aug 2011. Available from: https://www.youtube.com/watch?v=u0DMaydBOxk

Chapter 2

Dimensions of a Brand

In Greek mythology, Cassandra, the astoundingly beautiful daughter of Queen Hecuba and Priam, the King of Troy, often attracted the attention of men. Struck by her blinding beauty, Apollo, the god of healing, medicine, archery, music and poetry, bestowed the gift of prophecy upon her. Cassandra, however, aroused his anger when she resisted his romantic advances, and in a fit of fury, Apollo gave her the curse that she would always suffer the frustration and despair of people not paying heed to her prophecies and predictions.

In Homer's epic poems *The Odyssey* and *The Iliad*, Cassandra foresaw the destruction of Troy and warned the Trojan army saying, 'Beware of Danaos (Greeks) bearing gifts.' She pleaded with them not to bring in the wooden horse that the Greeks had installed outside the gates of Troy, as that would be the beginning of the destruction of Troy. But alas, Apollo's curse played out to perfection as nobody paid heed to her advice.

They brought the wooden horse (in which the Greek soldiers hid) inside the walls of Troy, and in the battle that ensued, Troy fell to the Greeks.

This phenomenon, where a person's perfectly logical and legitimate warnings or concerns are cast aside by others, came to be known as 'the Cassandra syndrome'.

Cassandra was, of course, a mythical character, but let's see how Ignaz Semmelweis,[1] a young Hungarian physician who worked in the General Hospital in Vienna, was stuck by this syndrome in 1846. Semmelweis was grappling with a strange problem that he had noticed in the two maternity wards in the hospital—the first staffed by all male doctors and the second managed by female midwives. He observed that the death rate of patients in the first ward was five times higher than in the second. Deeply puzzled, he tried hard to nail down the reason, but to no avail.

Then one day a doctor in the hospital died soon after conducting an autopsy during which he happened to prick his finger. Semmelweis immediately connected the dots. He discerned that the male doctors, who often conducted autopsies, carried the infection from the procedure on their hands and transmitted it to the patients in the maternity wards while examining them. Since the other ward was handled by midwives, who did not conduct autopsies, there was no associated infection, which explained the difference in the death rates between the two wards.

He was convinced that the doctors could easily disinfect their hands after an autopsy by washing them with a solution of chlorinated lime. In fact, he successfully experimented with a few doctors and obtained very encouraging results—the mortality rate in the ward fell by 90 per cent! Subsequently, armed with concrete evidence, he advocated that all doctors disinfect their hands with chlorine after completing autopsies. His colleagues, however, were not convinced and refused to acknowledge his logic, backed as it was with empirical evidence, for various reasons—it went against the grain of the established medical and scientific beliefs of the time, they did not want to be ordered around by a colleague, adapting to anything new is difficult and they did not want to take the blame for the patients' deaths.

As Semmelweis became increasingly vociferous in promoting sanitation, he suffered a nervous breakdown and was admitted to an asylum by a colleague. On one occasion, he was badly wounded when beaten up by an asylum guard. With infection creeping into his wound, it soon became gangrenous, and thereafter, at age 47, he succumbed to the infected wound just like the women who had lost their lives in the maternity ward. Today, of course, Semmelweis is acknowledged as a pioneer of antiseptic procedures and described as the 'saviour of mothers'.

With all the empirical evidence backing his perfectly legitimate claim, why was Semmelweis unable to show the light of reason to the medical fraternity? Why was he unsuccessful in convincing his colleagues about the merit of hygiene and its crucial role in sustaining life?

Such instances are not uncommon at the workplace.

You are convinced that your organization's enterprise data warehouse is in dire need of an upgradation which would address all the ills that the system currently suffers from—lack of agility and transparency in data transformation, data duplication and the swiftly running out storage capacity. You make a thoroughly researched, carefully thought-out presentation, backed by solid data to prove your point. The committee comprising your peers and three senior management members reject the proposal without much discussion.

You desperately need two additional headcounts in your team as the recent customer satisfaction survey has highlighted certain gaps in services which, in your opinion, cannot be addressed with the current resources. One of your team members is out on maternity leave and the others are just too stretched. You make an emotional plea at the departmental meeting, vividly describing the travails of the customers and the risk that this posed to business. Your pleas fall on deaf ears.

You go to the performance review round table meeting armed with data and anecdotal evidence, confident of arguing the case for promoting your team lead. The panel asks some uncomfortable questions and you get a nasty feeling that they are in sync about your candidate 'not being ready' for promotion this year.

You just fail to understand why such unfair and impractical targets have been thrust upon you especially in the wake of the overall economic slowdown. 'Are they out of their minds?' you scream mentally. Alas, the light of reason seems to have escaped them completely.

So, what does it take to obtain budgets for upgrading software, get a nod for an additional headcount, a promotion for a team member or business targets that are fair and realistic? The short answer is that you need political savviness.

A case in point is Lalit Modi,[2] the former Indian Premier League (IPL) boss. Struck by the astronomical revenues raked in by the American sports leagues, during his undergraduate days at the Duke University, Modi, the scion of the well-known Modi business family, had the vision of launching a professional cricket league in cricket-crazy India. He knew that this would necessarily entail a concerted interplay of four functions—entertainment, marketing, licensing and television. Upon his return to India in

1991, therefore, he embarked upon a tireless course of learning the ropes of these functions. He established the Modi Entertainment Network as a joint venture with the Walt Disney Company. He then facilitated their passage to India by helping them get into broadcast television and, in the process, mastered the nuts and bolts of their business. Later, he established a joint venture with the American television broadcaster, ESPN. Over time, he became a catalyst in catapulting the situation where the Board of Control for Cricket in India (BCCI) would give Doordarshan (an autonomous broadcaster owned by the Broadcasting Ministry of India) a fee to broadcast cricket, into a scenario where BCCI would grant exclusive rights to broadcast live cricket to a broadcaster for a handsome fee.

He pitched his idea of the Indian Cricket League, a cricket tournament in a new, one-day, 50-over format, to BCCI. His proposal was that he would own the league, the matches would be played amongst city-based teams, ESPN would get the rights to broadcast matches and BCCI would earn a fat royalty. Sadly, BCCI was not excited, and it turned down his proposal.

Unfazed by the refusal and determined more than ever to achieve his goal, Modi altered his strategy. He realized that he needed to work from inside rather than outside the BCCI. Over the next 12 years, Modi worked relentlessly, building alliances and striking coalitions to get a foothold on the BCCI board. In 1999, he got elected to the Himachal Pradesh Cricket Association, but that was short lived, as he had to step down shortly thereafter, after he fell out with the local officials. In 2004, leveraging his political contacts, he ousted the Rungta family to gain control of the Rajasthan Cricket Association. Subsequently, in 2005, Modi joined hands with the National Congress Party leader Sharad Pawar to defeat Jagmohan Dalmiya in the BCCI presidential elections. When Sharad Pawar stepped in as the BCCI president, he inducted Modi as one of the five vice presidents. Shortly thereafter, in 2008, Modi received a cheque of $25 million from the president of BCCI to launch the IPL.

Modi had achieved his goal. While Modi was able to sell the worthiness of his idea leading to the successful launch of the IPL, Semmelweis was thumped by the Cassandra syndrome. He was unable to convince the medical fraternity to adopt his idea which had the potential to save millions of lives. One of the reasons why Lalit Modi was able to achieve his goal was his political acumen and robust connections in the corporate and political circles which strengthened his impact and influence. Dr Semmelweis, on the other hand, was unable to garner support for his legitimately valid claim, for lack of allies.

What does it take to be heard, to have people take you seriously, be receptive to your ideas, supportive of your strategy and, in general, be positively disposed towards you? The answer lies in your personal credibility, represented by a powerful brand, which also incorporates your ability to understand and navigate through the organization's political dynamics.

Navigating through the Political Landscape

The word 'politics' or 'political' is often perceived as negative. It is associated with manipulation, that is, seeking or taking credit for something that is not rightfully yours or walking over people to push your own agenda to the detriment of the group and the organization. It is reminiscent of Niccolò Machiavelli, the 15th-century Italian diplomat and writer of *The Prince*, a political commentary on leveraging ruthless and self-serving cunning for grabbing and retaining power. In fact, the term 'Machiavellian' is considered derogatory as it represents unscrupulous actions in the domain of politics.

An executive, who had been recently been laid off, was heard exclaiming, 'I could not survive the office politics!' A parent recently spoke to me about how miserable his son was at office because 'he does not know how to play politics.' And a short time ago, a former colleague confided in me saying 'how hor-rendously political the organization had become.' Office poli-tics are clearly considered vile, to be circumvented or steered clear of.

However, circumventing or sidestepping these dynamics or considering yourself above them is not only naive, it is certainly not a formula for success. It would be prudent to acknowledge the organization's political landscape, engage in it constructively and leverage it to garner support for achieving your own goals and those of the organization. Besides, politics need not be dirty, manipulative and negative.

Defining Politics

Think of an organization where people and departments are seamlessly aligned, they co-operate with each other to perfection, with each one having access to resources like time, budget, manpower and information. This is nothing short of utopia, the illusionary place embodying a perfect society, described by Thomas More in a socio-political satire published in 1516.

In reality, however, conflict and competition are built into the organizational structure for three reasons.

Scarcity of Resources

Three teams need an additional headcount, with each team looking upon its need as more critical than that of the other two. The organizational budget, on the other hand, allows sanctioning just one. How will this scenario play out? Teams are likely to vie with each other to influence the decision-makers into pronouncing the verdict in its favour. Similarly, teams constantly compete for other resources like space, budgets, assignments, projects and even the boss's attention.

Interdependence

While teams compete for resources, they also depend on each other for inputs and information to turn out timely and quality deliverables. Engaged in driving their own agendas, teams often find themselves at the crossroads of conflict because of this interdependence.

Diversity

People not only have conflicting goals and priorities, they also differ on several other dimensions like personality, working style, culture, gender and generation. Conflict is triggered when people operate on different wavelengths along these multifarious dimensions.

Painting these on a single canvas turns out a picture laden with dynamic pulls and pushes, shoves and nudges, representing varying shades of organizational politics. We are already thrown into this game since this is the environment we have chosen to be in. It would be judicious to acknowledge it and engage in it intelligently and ethically to drive one's personal and organizational goals. 'Man is by nature a political animal,' was the astute observation of the 4th century BC Greek philosopher, Aristotle, in his book, *Politics*.

Being Politically Savvy

Simon Baddeley and Kim James[3] have defined an interesting framework to categorize people based on their savviness in engaging in the organization's political dynamics. The framework is based on two dimensions—goal alignment and political acumen.

Goal alignment refers to the motivation or the propensity of a person to act fairly and in the interest of the overall organizational goals, rather than acting out of narrow self-interest.

Figure 2.1. The Political-savvy Framework

Source: Adapted from 'Owl, Fox, Donkey or Sheep: Political Skills for Managers' by Simon Baddeley and Kim James.

Political acumen is defined as a person's ability to discern the organization's political landscape and perceive the less-obvious dynamics in terms of the where power resides, how people are aligned, the way decisions are made and the stated and unstated agendas of different groups.

Four profiles emerge at the intersection of these two parameters.

Quadrant 1: Low Goal Alignment + High Political Acumen

Symbolized by a *Fox*

- Politically intelligent people operating in Quadrant 1 are tuned to the organizational dynamics. Frequently donning a mask, they are reluctant to disclose information and their true feelings and opinions. Smooth and cunning, they often manipulate situations to their advantage and their propensity to prioritize self over group and organizational interest, tend to bring themselves short-term wins but impede long-term success.

Quadrant 2: High Goal Alignment + High Political Acumen

Symbolized by an *Owl*

- Politically intelligent, Quadrant 2 operators are aware of who calls the shots and how decisions are made in the organization. They leverage their social skills to engage with people and focus on building constructive relationships which hold them in good stead when they need to garner support for driving their agenda. Motivated by the larger organizational interest, they are known to act ethically and with integrity. Considered wise, they are respected by their colleagues.

Quadrant 3: High Goal Alignment + Low Political Acumen

Symbolized by *Sheep*

- Oblivious of the political dynamics in terms of the way things work and where the power lies, people operating in Quadrant 3 are considered naive and under-political. They are liked by people on account of their open and friendly disposition and because they act ethically in the interest of the larger group. But they are unable to achieve their goals as they have not invested in building strategic relationships essential to influence decisions and gain support.

Quadrant 4: Low Goal Alignment + Low Political Acumen

Symbolized by *Donkey*

- Quadrant 4 operators are neither conversant with the organizational landscape, nor do they have the astuteness and the social skills for building a supportive ecosystem. They are out for themselves and are likely to act out of self-interest.

Clearly, people with a high degree of political acumen and goal alignment, who typically operate in the second Quadrant of this framework are well poised for achieving their goals and success in influencing decisions, obtaining resources, being considered for career-enhancing opportunities and having a voice at the table. They embody a powerful brand characterized by impact and influence, an ability to discern and engage constructively and ethically in the organization's political dynamics, an aptitude for forging constructive relationships, the acumen for building a robust network and the capacity to present themselves impactfully and appropriately in different situations.

Introspection: Are You Politically Savvy?

Take the political skills assessment below, scoring each question on a 5-point scale, where:

1 = Strongly disagree
2 = Disagree
3 = Neutral (neither agree nor disagree)
4 = Agree
5 = Strongly agree

Table 2.1: Self Assessment: Are You Politically Savvy?

S.N.	Parameter	Score
	Trust	
1	I am authentic in my dealings with people.	
2	People trust my sincerity.	
3	People recognize me for my knowledge, skills and the ability to deliver results.	
	Social intelligence	
4	I observe people closely.	
5	I am a good listener and I pay attention to both the person's words and body language.	
6	I read people well and am able to discern their motivations and agendas.	
7	I communicate well with people.	
8	People feel comfortable when interacting with me.	
9	I am usually successful in influencing people and situations.	
	Networking	
10	I think networking is important and I intentionally allocate time to networking.	
11	I have a knack for building rapport with people.	
12	I have a well-rounded network which I can leverage for rallying allies when needed.	
13	I am well connected with influential people whose support I can count on.	
14	My network serves me well to keep me abreast of organizational information.	

- Add up your score for all the statements and divide by 14 to get your political-savvy score.

- Interpretation:

  o 4 or 5—high political skills

  o 3—need to develop your political skills

  o 1 or 2—low political skills

The three elements of political skills—trust, social intelligence and networking—align well with the four dimensions of a personal brand described below.

Four Dimensions of a Personal Brand

While a brand as a concept is nebulous, easier felt and sensed but difficult to nail down, it would be pertinent to define it broadly in terms of the following four dimensions.

Figure 2.2. The Four Dimensions of a Personal Brand

Substance

Substance, the first dimension and the fulcrum of your brand, represents your expertise and core skills in terms of your business acumen, domain knowledge, experience, qualification, ideas, initiative and the ability to solve problems and make sound decisions. It needs to be developed and shaped not only in the context of your current role, but also the one that you are aspiring for in the near and medium horizon. Additionally, and more importantly, it embodies your principles and personal moral line, and the consistency with which you stand by them in different situations.

Substance, therefore, reflects the perception of your stakeholders in terms of your genuineness, authenticity, sincerity and your propensity to prioritize group or organizational interest over self-interest, in addition to their confidence in your expertise and ability to deliver results.

Connect

This alludes to your social capital or the web of relationships that you have built over time. It can open the doors for advocacy, mentorship, resources, information, camaraderie and friendship that are crucial for both your career progression as well as for a meaningful and balanced life. Consider these scenarios:

- You connect a friend who is seeking a job change with consultants and other professionals with whom he can explore job opportunities.

- Your department needs some market intelligence while laying down certain internal policies and you are able to get the required information through your industry connections.

- You are in the know with respect to the general organizational environment and the underlying dynamics that are at play.

- You are successful in influencing a decision in your favour as a result of being able to rally allies for your cause.

In all the above scenarios, you come across as a valuable and well-networked person. Your credibility is enhanced, and your brand stands augmented.

Your competence in striking constructive relationships rests upon your ability to engage with people and handle difficult interpersonal situations, which calls for a constellation of skills like social adeptness, emotional intelligence and political savviness.

Visibility

Just as a product brand derives its strength from judicious marketing communication and advertisement, in the same vein, a personal brand, too, draws its muscle from visibility. It is just as important to communicate your substance, comprising your knowledge, skills and achievements, to your stakeholders, as it is to constantly enhance it and keep it current. The logic is simple. How will your stakeholders appreciate and recognize your good work and give you credit for it unless they know about it? It is imperative, therefore, to promote your substance by creating a well thought out messaging around it, in a manner that is responsible, focused and devoid of pompousness and trumpet blowing.

Wrapping

We are often told 'don't judge a book by its cover.' But don't we all? So, a pertinent question to mull over is—how inviting is your wrapping in terms of your demeanour, communicating style, confidence and mannerisms? What impressions do people take away when they meet you? Is your wrapping striking enough to persuade people to take a step forward and explore your substance, or does it dissuade them from discovering the knowledge, skills and the value that resides within you? It is important, therefore, to don a wrapping that is attractive and interesting, which strengthens, rather than diminishes, your brand.

The four dimensions need to work in tandem for rendering a brand strong and compelling. We will explore the four dimensions of a powerful personal brand—substance, connect, visibility and wrapping—in the following chapters.

- Apart from cognitive skills, you need to be politically savvy to be able to navigate through the organization's political dynamics to drive your agenda and achieve your goals.

- The political dynamics emanate from conflict and competition that are built into the fabric of an organization. There are three reasons for this.

  o Scarcity of resources

  o Interdependence for achieving goals that are often conflicting and incompatible

  o Diversity of perspective and working styles

- Political savviness is about understanding the organization's political landscape in terms of where the power resides, how decisions are made and the way people are aligned, on the one hand, and the ability to navigate constructively through these dynamics, on the other. This calls for an assortment of skills like:

  o Trustworthiness

  o Social intelligence

  o Networking

- These skills align strongly with the four dimensions of a powerful brand:

  o **Substance:** This is the mainstay of your brand that rests on your professional skills, domain knowledge and the ability to deliver results, as well as your propensity to do the right thing and engage ethically.

  o **Connect:** This constitutes your ability to connect with people, forge constructive relationships and build a robust network.

  o **Visibility:** This constitutes your strategy for communicating your strengths, talents and achievements to your stakeholders, to enable them to account for these when making decisions that impact you and your career.

  o **Wrapping:** This is your brand's outermost layer encompassing your demeanour, communication style, confidence and mannerisms. It is important to develop a wrapping that is appealing and encourages people to come forward and explore your substance.

- The four dimensions work in concert to build a powerful brand that assists you in steering your career in the desired direction.

References

1. Kadar N, Romero R, Papp Z. Ignaz Semmelweis: the 'Savior of Mothers'. Am J Obstet Gynecol [Internet]. 1 Dec 2018;219(6):519–22. Available from: https://www.ajog.org/article/S0002-9378(18)30943-8/fulltext

2. Kohli R. The launch of the Indian Premier League. Columbia Business School, Columbia CaseWorks [Internet]. 20 March 2009. Available from: https://www0.gsb.columbia.edu/mygsb/faculty/research/pubfiles/5179/IPL.pdf

3. Baddeley S, James K. Management learning, owl, fox, donkey or sheep: political skills for managers [Internet]. SAGE Publications. 1 April 1987. Available from: https://journals.sagepub.com/doi/10.1177/135050768701800101

Substance

The First Dimension

Chapter 3

Doing the
Right Thing

Substance, the essence of your brand, defines its reliability, trustworthiness and authenticity. It encompasses two elements. The first, and the most important, element is the strength of character outlined by your fundamental principles and personal code of ethics, and the way these manifest themselves in your decisions and judgment calls in different personal and professional situations, especially those marked by high pressure and high stakes. Do you stand by your principles even at the expense of your personal performance? Can you own up to a mistake? Are you courageous enough to take the right, not the easy, call in a tough situation?

The second element that defines your substance is your professional competence. It incorporates your domain knowledge, technical expertise and qualification, and your effectiveness in applying these in different work scenarios with initiative, drive and out-of-box thinking.

Doing the Right Thing Is Always in Vogue

We often find ourselves at the crossroads of difficult choices. Whether to do or not to do? Whether to respond to the call of expediency and opt for the seemingly accelerated path towards a goal, or brace oneself for the long, arduous haul that the principle endorses? It helps to listen to your intuition when faced with dilemmas such as these, for deep down your gut you know what is right, even when the rational mind might dither and try to lure you to the path of a quick win.

The idea 'doing the right thing is always the right thing', propounded by entrepreneur, speaker and internet personality, Gary Vaynerchuk, is indeed powerful. When faced with a quandary, ruminate on this idea. Ponder over it. Embrace it. Listen to what feels right for you. Take a pause to think over, instead of rushing into an impulsive action, for this will show you the light and lead you to the right decision. Acting with integrity can be hard, as it may imply losing something or not getting something that you desire, but letting expediency triumph over principle is not a strategy for long-term success and eventual peace.

In the book *How Will You Measure Your Life?*,[1] co-author and Harvard Business School professor, Clayton M. Christensen makes a powerful statement that adhering to your personal moral line 100 per cent of the time is easier than 98 per cent, because if you justify crossing it once, nothing stops you from crossing it again. When faced with a tough choice, either in personal or professional life, it is easy to succumb with the thought that it is okay to go ahead just this one time, given the 'extenuating circumstance'. But as it turns out, life is about a series of 'extenuating circumstances'. And the price of doing something 'just this once' may seem minuscule in that moment, but eventually, the full cost is colossal as it turned out for Nick Leeson, Jerry del Missier and Rajat Gupta.

Less serious acts of transgression like cheating on expense reports, pinching office stationery, using the office telecommunication infrastructure for making personal, long-distance calls or taking undue advantage of generous sick leave policies don't go unnoticed either. Such deeds, by taking the sheen off your substance, stand to mitigate your brand.

Just This Once

Nick Leeson[2] has been variously described as 'brilliant', 'a high-flyer who liked to dabble in dare-devil trades' as well as a 'rogue trader'. Leeson has to his credit the dubious distinction of driving Barings, one the most reputable financial institutions of the United Kingdom, to bankruptcy in 1995. This was touted as one of the biggest financial scandals of the 20th century in which 1,200 employees lost their jobs; Leeson was sentenced to a six and a half years in prison and Barings was sold to ING, the Dutch bank, for a mere £1.00.

Leeson had been deputed to manage Barings's derivates trade on the Singapore exchange in 1992. Spurred by some early and quick wins, he started engaging in increasingly risky, highly speculative, but enormously remunerative trades, soon earning the reputation of being a market mover and shaker. In 1992, he contributed almost 10 per cent to the bank's total profits; thus securing the trust of his superiors who started perceiving him as a very valuable and near infallible asset.

His winning streak, however, proved to be a shooting star when a while later he made a few market calls that did not play out quite as expected, bringing in huge losses. He tried to compensate for the losses by taking even riskier positions. And then there was no turning back as he was drawn deeper and deeper into the whirlpool of fraud and deceit, forging documents, covering documents and hiding losses in an obscure 'error account'. By 1994, his total accumulated losses of more than 208 million pounds, amounted to more than half the bank's capital. The 233-year old institution filed for bankruptcy on February 26, 1995.

Leeson's brand stood eroded, falling severely short on sound judgement. He earned the reputation for being a highly knowledgeable, competent gambler, devoid of the wisdom to decide when to put the brakes, a coward who chose to resort to deception, instead of owning up his transgression, coming out clean and facing the consequences.

Inability or Avoidance?

'How could such a boringly competent, intelligent and proficient guy get embroiled in such a situation?' is the question that Jerry del Missier's[3] former colleagues struggle to answer to this day. Del Missier, the resoundingly successful banker, credited with helping build the highly remunerative investment banking arm of the British financial giant—Barclays, fell to disgrace in the face of the London Interbank Offered Rate (LIBOR) scandal. (LIBOR is a key interest rate that serves as a benchmark for global borrowing. The British Bankers' Association derives this rate daily by inviting a panel of the world's largest financial institutions to submit the rate at which they would be willing to borrow funds. These are then averaged out to get LIBOR.)

Investigations in the aftermath of the 2008 economic meltdown found that during the period 2005 to 2007, Barclays' derivative traders had worked in complicity with the company's rate submitters to feed artificially high or low rates into LIBOR, thus manipulating the rate to benefit whatever positions they held in the market. This discovery triggered a colossal scandal in 2012 for which Barclays had to pay a whopping 290 million pounds as fine, and Jerry del Missier, along with his boss and the then CEO, Robert Diamond, were shown the door, bringing their glittering careers to a disgraceful and dramatic end.

What had triggered this?

On 29 October 2008, Diamond, the then head of the investment banking division, had a telephonic conversation with the deputy governor of the Bank of England, Paul Tucker, who at some point said, 'It did not always need to be the case that Barclays's LIBOR submissions be so high.' Soon after the call, Diamond wrote the message in a note and relayed it to the CEO, John Varley, with a copy to del Missier.

During the investigations that followed, Diamond maintained that he had not interpreted Tucker's comment as an implicit indication to submit a lower rate. But del Missier did. And on his instructions the bank submitters started to do so. In his testimony during the investigations, del Missier cut a sorry figure when he said that he was 'merely following Diamond's instructions to lowball LIBOR'!

This response speaks volumes about Jerry del Missier and can be construed as one of the following based on how you look at it.

- *Incompetent* if you think that he had acted without realizing that his action was tantamount to manipulation, representing a serious breach of any code of conduct. Given his immaculate track record, this seems unlikely.

- *Weak and cowardly* if you think that he lacked the courage and boldness to push back and spell out the implications of the instructions he had received from his boss.

- *Unethical* if you think that he had acted with full awareness.

Whatever the case may be, Jerry del Missier's stature stands eroded and his brand tarnished. His moral compass seems to have not quite pointed true north.

Flawed Judgement

Orphaned in his teens, Rajat Gupta[4] made it to IIT Delhi and then to Harvard Business School on full scholarship, soon after which he joined the elite management consulting firm McKinsey & Company. McKinsey had initially rejected Gupta on account of inadequate work experience but had reversed the decision when his Harvard professor, Walter J. Salmon, had intervened by speaking to Ron Daniel, the then head of McKinsey's New York office. His meteoric rise in the company in a very competitive environment is legendary. It culminated in his appointment to the corner office in 1994, when Gupta broke through the racial glass ceiling to become McKinsey's first managing director born outside the USA. From there on he became the toast of the corporate world, rubbing shoulders with CEOs and heads of states.

Gupta was a much sought-after person for corporate board positions when he retired from McKinsey in 2007, after heading it for nine years. Gupta soon joined the boards of Goldman Sachs, Procter & Gamble, American Airlines and Harvard Business School.

Gupta's fall from grace commenced in 2010 amid the investigations of the Sri Lankan hedge fund manager, Raj Rajaratnam, as a part of the US government's onslaught on insider trading. On that fateful day in September 2008, the Goldman Sachs directors were informed during the board meeting that Warren Buffett's Berkshire Hathaway was investing $5 billion in Goldman Sachs, and that this would go a long way in strengthening the much-needed public confidence in the firm. A minute after the meeting ended, someone called Rajaratnam from Gupta's phone, tipping him on the impending investment. Rajaratnam was quick to buy Goldman Sachs stocks before this news was made public, raking up $800,000 in less than 24 hours.

Even though nothing concrete was found, the circumstantial evidence was strong enough to point to Gupta's guilt, who was sentenced to two years of imprisonment for leaking the boardroom secrets of Goldman Sachs. And with that his brand came crashing down.

Pointing True North

'With integrity, you have nothing to fear, since you have nothing to hide. With integrity, you will do the right thing, so you will have no guilt,' says Zig Ziglar, author of *Over the Top: Moving from Survival to Stability, from Stability to Success, from Success to Significance.*

Consider the stories below where people displayed tremendous character through their ethical calls, sometimes at the expense of their personal performance and attainment of goals. Though not always easy, acting with integrity and the concomitant feeling of having done the right thing not only brings you immense calm and satisfaction but also renders you trustworthy; thereby enhancing your reputation and lending tremendous power to your brand.

The year was 2001. A tough year! With the Indian economy growing at a meagre 4.8 per cent, business had not been great. The outgoing CEO of an advertising company was faced with an ethical dilemma. He had the option of carrying out advance billing for a few projects, thereby leaving behind a healthy balance sheet as legacy, or abandoning the idea of advance billing and leaving on a note of loss and non-performance. The CEO chose to do the latter and, in taking this course, demonstrated his propensity to do the right thing. And in doing so, he earned the reputation of one who could be trusted to act with integrity and make the right judgement calls, thereby adding the strong muscles of reliability and trustworthiness to his brand.

****

Australian cricketer Adam Gilchrist is considered one of the greatest wicketkeepers–batsmen in the history of the game. The world of cricket has undoubtedly been bowled over by his outstanding wicket keeping and suave batting strokes. But the world remembers him more for an act that left people truly speechless and awestruck. During the World Cup of Australia–Sri Lanka semi-finals in 2003, Gilchrist walked out to the pavilion, even though the umpire had given him not out to an appeal by Aravinda de Silva. 'Something inside me said "walk" so I went,' he later said in an interview.[5]

****

On the fifth day of the Australia–England centenary test played in 1977 to mark the 100th anniversary of the first test match between the two countries, the English batsman Derek Randall was going great guns at 161, when umpire Tony Brooks gave him out to a catch by Rodney Marsh, the Australian wicketkeeper. But in a genuine display of sportsmanship, Marsh indicated to the umpire that his catch was not clean, thereby becoming instrumental in having Randall return to the crease.[6]

****

At a cross-country racing event held at Burlada in Spain in 2012, Kenyan runner Abel Mutai was leading the race. He stopped 100 meters short of the finish line erroneously thinking that he had completed the race. Spanish runner, Iván Fernández Anaya, who had just caught up with Mutai, had the big opportunity to run past him to seize the gold, but guess what? He cautioned Mutai about the finish line still being some distance away and signalled to him to keep going. 'I did what I had to do. He was the rightful winner. I didn't deserve to win,' he later said in an interview to the Spanish newspaper, El País, eliciting a loud applause and a unanimous endorsement from people the world over.[7]

****

In another display of authentic sportsmanship, during the Golden Jubilee Test played between India and England in 1980, bowler Kapil Dev and wicketkeeper Syed Kirmani had made a strong appeal for a caught behind stumps for batsman Bob Taylor. Umpire Hanumantha Rao responded to the appeal by raising his finger. But Bob Taylor was not convinced. Neither was captain

Gundappa Viswanath, who was fielding at slips. Certain that Taylor's bat had not touched the ball, Viswanath spoke to the umpire and got him to reverse his decision. This one virtuous act won him many hearts, even though India eventually lost the match.[8]

Acting with Courage

Madhu Khatri, former general counsel at Wipro and Microsoft, said,

One's personal brand is built by putting a stake in the ground for what you stand for. That's not always easy because life is not always black and white. There's a lot of gray and ambiguity. And through that ambiguity your stakeholders should be able to count on you to be objective and fearless. And that to my mind is the bedrock of a brand.

Consider the following examples.

Walking the Talk

David Mackenzie Ogilvy, the British advertising legend who founded Ogilvy & Mather, the renowned advertising, marketing and public relations agency, had famously said, 'However able they may be, ambitious people won't stay in outfits which practice nepotism. This is one mistake I did not make; my son is in the real estate business, secure in the knowledge that he owes nothing of his success to his father.' He walked the talk and lived by his principle of 'no nepotism' by keeping his son out of his multi-million dollar advertising company. David Fairfield Ogilvy, his son, went on to make a successful career in the real-estate business. This one act of courage has added a unique flavour of 'doing the right thing' to David Ogilvy's brand.

Being True to Your Cause

Chetna Vasishth, who runs ChetChat, a career and education chat show, says

My viewer is the most important entity in my eco-system and all my energies and actions are oriented towards building and reinforcing their trust. I, therefore, maintain very exacting standards around the message I deliver to my young and impressionable viewers. While revenue is important, and sponsorship is the mainstay of revenue, I have turned down lucrative offers from potential sponsors whenever I have felt that their product or message was either not relevant, or might compromise the interest of my viewer.

It takes courage and a compass pointing true north to do this.

Owning Up

'I had committed the indiscretion of inadvertently revealing confidential company information to the media a couple of decades ago. Owning up this impropriety, I had put in my papers. But my resignation was turned down by the management,' a senior executive with a stellar corporate career recently shared with me. Owning up a transgression is again an act of courage.

Soliciting Divergent Views

Legend has it that the renowned automobile executive, Lido Anthony 'Lee' Iacocca, who is credited with developing some of the iconic, best-selling brands like Mustang and Pinto while at the Ford Motor Company in the 1960s, and reviving the Chrysler Corporation as its CEO during the 1980s, once shocked people when he fired his vice president. When asked as to why he had taken such a drastic action towards a person with whom he got along so well, seldom had a disagreement with and who had supported his ideas and actions on every occasion, he had responded, 'That's just the point. Why should I pay a huge salary to a man who always has my opinion?' When it is so convenient to have people around you who are aligned and in agreement, welcoming, and even soliciting dissent, is an act of courage.

Being Forgiving

> *The weak can never forgive. Forgiveness is the attribute of the strong.*
> —*Mahatma Gandhi*

Nelson Mandela emerged from his tiny jail cell where he had spent 30 years, ready to forgive those who had put him there, and in doing so, he ignited and inspired a nation that had been torn apart by apartheid for 50 long years. His spirit of forgiveness is vividly depicted in *Invictus*, the biographical film based on John Carlin's book *Playing the Enemy: Nelson Mandela and the Game that made a Nation*.

The end of apartheid in South Africa marked its return to international sports. Set to host the Rugby World Cup in 1995, the South African international rugby union team, Springboks, gained an automatic entry into the tournament as the host team. The Blacks opposed the team since it symbolized White supremacy. In fact, in a pre-tournament match with England, they cheered England and jeered Springboks. Recognizing this chasm and determined to address it, Mandela engineered a meeting between the newly formed, Black dominated South African Sports Committee and the Springboks team. He urged them to collaborate and play as one, as he strongly believed that a Springboks victory in the World Cup would go a long way in uniting and inspiring the nation and dispelling apartheid in spirit.

Starting off as an underdog, Springboks went on to score miraculous victories against Australia, France and New Zealand as the entire nation, motivated by Mandela's own spirit of forgiveness, united to support their team. Much to the nation's delight,

Springboks raised the William Webb Ellis Cup, handed to them by Mandela himself.

The ability to let go of the past and make a new beginning calls for strength, and this strength is reflected in your brand.

Thus, walking the talk by demonstrating the principles that you advocate, coming clean by owning up a transgression, turning down the lure of material gains in the interest of the cause that you stand for, soliciting divergent and contradictory views and forgiving those who have wronged you are examples of courageous acts that evoke trust, strengthen your substance and are central to a strong brand.

CALL FOR ACTION

Introspection

1. Think of the time when you cut a corner, allowing expediency to overshadow principle by acting in a way that did not feel quite right.

   • How did it feel?

   • What was the immediate result?

   • What was the long-term result?

   • How did it impact your brand?

2. Think of the time when you allowed principle to triumph over expediency by acting in a way that felt right but diminished your performance at that moment.

   • How did it feel?

   • What was the immediate result?

   • What was the long-term result?

   • How did it impact your brand?

PERSONAL BRANDING TIPS

- Substance, the bedrock of your brand, embodies your reliability, trustworthiness and authenticity.

- It comprises two elements. First, your strength of character defined by your fundamental principles and the way these manifest in your decisions. Second, your professional competence encompassing your knowledge, skills and business acumen and your effectiveness in applying these in different work scenarios.

- 'Doing the right thing is always the right thing.' Taking a pause to ponder over this idea, when faced with an ethical dilemma, will help you circumvent the temptation of expediency and do what feels right deep down your gut.

- Doing the right thing may not always be easy, but doing so will give you a sense of calm, render you trustworthy, enhance your reputation and lend power to your brand.

References

1. Christensen C, Allworth J, Dillon K. How will you figure out your life? New York City, NY: Harper Business; 2012.
2. Rodrogues J.. Barings collapse at 20: how rogue trader Nick Leeson broke the bank. The Guardian [Internet]. 24 Feb 2015. Available from: https://www.theguardian.com/business/from-the-archive-blog/2015/feb/24/nick-leeson-barings-bank-1995-20-archive
3. MailOnline [Internet]. The phone-call that 'led to rate-rigging': Barclays release details of conversation with Bank of England man. 3 July 2012. Available from: https://www.dailymail.co.uk/news/article-2168242/Barclays-release-details-Bank-England-man-says-led-Libor-rigging.html
4. Hindu BusinessLine [Internet]. Rajat Gupta—a corporate honcho's stunning fall from grace. 12 March 2018. Available from: https://www.thehindubusinessline.com/markets/rajat-gupta-a-corporate-honchos-stunning-fall-from-grace/article20519052.ece

5. Cricketer [Internet]. World Cup moments no. 25: Adam Gilchrist walks the walk. 16 May 2019. Available from:https://www.thecricketer.com/Topics/australia/world_cup_moments_no25_adam_gilchrist_walks_the_walk.html

6. BBC Sports [Internet]. Randall recalls centenary fireworks. 12 March 2002. Available from: http://news.bbc.co.uk/sport2/hi/cricket/1867342.stm

7. HuffPost [Internet]. Ivan Fernandez Anaya, Spanish runner, intentionally loses race so opponent can win. 6 Dec 2017. Available from: https://www.huffpost.com/entry/ivan-fernandez-anaya-hone_n_2505360

8. News 18 [Internet]. 19th February 1980: Botham eclipses Viswanath's sportsmanship in Golden Jubilee test. 19 Feb 2019. Available from: https://www.news18.com/cricketnext/news/19th-february-1980-botham-eclipses-viswanaths-sportsmanship-in-golden-jubilee-test-2040735.html#:~:text=Cricket%20Home%20%C2%BB%20News-,19th%20February%201980%3A%20Botham%20Eclipses%20Viswanath's%20Sportsmanship%20in%20Golden%20Jubilee,hosts%2C%20with%20bat%20and%20ball.

Chapter 4

Building Your Professional Competence

Professional competence is the second critical component of 'Substance', the first dimension of a powerful brand. It encompasses your knowledge, skills and abilities and your propensity to apply these judiciously in different work situations, in addition to your experience and track record in terms of your achievements as well as your failed efforts.

It would be prudent to think through your competencies with reference to the Four Stages of Contribution model presented in the 'Introduction'. Is your current set of competencies and skills likely to serve you well in your current role? Does it position you suitably for the role that you are aspiring for? People often transition into new roles and career stages by virtue of excelling in their current roles but are unable to discern the key competencies, skills and the mindset required for succeeding in the new role. Remaining deeply focused on deliverables and the concomitant technical and domain competencies, people tend to overlook the importance of developing an in-depth understanding of the business, the regulatory framework, current market trends, industry best practices and the softer skills like communicating, presenting, networking, influencing and relationship building, along with managerial and mentoring skills for leading and developing people and setting them up for success. As a result, they are unable to realize their full potential by doing complete justice to their enhanced roles.

It is important, therefore, to constantly add to your skills and reinvent your expertise in the context of your current and future roles, thereby rendering your brand relevant and marketable. The propensity to *learn constantly*, *being imaginative* and *being farsighted* will hold you in good stead as you traverse your career.

Being a Constant Learner

'It's what you learn after you know it all, that counts,' are the insightful words of the celebrated basketball coach, John Wooden, which couldn't be closer to truth in this highly dynamic, constantly changing world, where knowledge and skills are subject to rapid obsolescence. Inculcating the ability and the attitude to learn every moment is imperative, therefore, to succeed and stride towards your goals.

Expand Your Domain Knowledge

The year was 1994. A young BSc computer science graduate had a dream of working in the land of opportunity—the USA—riding on the Y2K wave. Y2K refers to the software applications bug associated with date transition, which was expected to bring down critical computer applications at the turn of the millennium. Companies across the world, in their quest for rendering their software Y2K compliant, were making a beeline to Indian IT companies, which, flush with projects, were having a field day rewriting code to fix this problem.

What stood between him and his dream, however, was his three-year BSc degree. He would do brilliantly in tests and interviews with the IT companies that rode on the Y2K band-wagon, but his degree was his nemesis that he had to con-stantly contend with, as only a 4-year degree was recognized in the USA. Going through this painful experience of facing repeated rejection, he resolved to up his game by augment-ing his knowledge. He was determined to be recognized for his superior technical skills, rather than being branded merely as a proficient 'Y2K coder'.

He started by investing in a 'PC-XT' computer and went on to code a series of programs to demonstrate his knowledge and competency in programming. For instance, leveraging the principles of physics, he wrote a program to present a 3D model of an aircraft taking off. Next, he wrote an application, a precursor of the present-day AutoCAD application, for gen-erating two-dimensional engineering drawings. He also wrote a program to present his CV in a graphical format, just like one would do using PowerPoint today. In effect, he had written an application with features very similar to PowerPoint! Needless to say that this entailed deep subject knowledge and a com-puting proficiency of a very high order.

He would go for interviews, armed with 12 such applications, loaded on a few floppies, and demonstrate his technical exper-tise on the computer, instead of just talking about it. He also altered his strategy for exploring the job market. He decided to apply to smaller, start-up companies that worked primarily with clients in Europe, where a 3-year degree was recognized.

*****

Chandra Sekhar A. K. N. R., Senior Vice President at a multi-national bank, got his first break at ASML Technologies Ltd.

Subsequently, he moved from strength to strength, getting opportunities to work on multiple technologies around the world, honing his technical skills and learning the ropes of working in diverse cultures along the way. Thus, instead of being discouraged by adversity, Chandra chose to overcome the roadblocks by building his brand as a technical expert par excellence.

Chandra's quest for knowledge continues to this day. In the last two years, he has taken 75 courses on topics as varied as macroeconomics, social and economic networks, money and banking, model thinking, supply chain management, debt sustainable analysis, financial programming and policies, and design thinking and public procurement on open online learning portals like Massive Open Online Courses. These portals offer online courses from top-notch institutions and companies like Harvard, MIT and Microsoft in a wide spectrum of subjects like computer science, data science, business and management amongst others.

Expand Your Functional Expertise

A couple of years into a recruitment role, Juhi Sharma was conversant with the full life cycle of the recruiting process comprising sourcing and screening candidates, engaging with hiring managers to understand requirements, coordinating candidate interviews, negotiating compensation and facilitating offer letters.

Making a conscious attempt to step out of her comfort zone, she applied for a role in the learning and development (L&D) vertical where a position had fallen vacant. Sharma was granted the role based on her proven track record as a stellar recruiter and a fast learner. In her new role, she equipped herself with courses in facilitation and psychometric assessments and started facilitating some basic training programs. Next, she engaged with experienced external trainers to design a strong leadership program for which she was commended by her stakeholders. She went on to launch a robust training calendar thereafter.

When the assistant to the HR head proceeded on maternity leave, Sharma offered to fill in her role, part time, in addition to her L&D responsibilities, taking on one intern to help her balance out the two roles. In her new role, she was tasked with preparing the monthly HR dashboard and assisting the HR head in preparing presentations for different forums. This gave her a well-rounded knowledge of the different HR verticals and an understanding of the key HR statistics.

Once she was relieved from this additional responsibility, in her quest to learn more about compensation and benefits, Sharma started investing half a day every week to sit down with the compensation and benefits executive to understand the application and the underlying process.

The HR head had also instituted a practice of job rotation with the intent to help people grow by gaining cross functional knowledge. Each person in the team had the option of playing a role of her choice within different HR verticals for one week. Taking advantage of this practice, Sharma opted for compensation and benefits to further solidify her knowledge in that area.

Having broadened her functional knowledge as a result of her initiative and drive, Sharma demonstrated strong commitment towards her professional development and became a valuable resource and a coveted team member. The adjective 'go-getter' stood firmly ensconced in her brand.

Broaden Your Skills

'While "knowledge" continues to be the bedrock of my brand, I now wanted to steer my brand from techno-functional expertise to a management-centric one, and my next stint with ANZ provided ample opportunity to do so,' says Chandra Sekhar A. K. N. R. Perceiving some rough edges in his manner of dealing with people, he now focused on sharpening his leadership skills. Chandra realized that understanding human psychology and the principles of people management were imperative to bring to fruition his goal to be a collaborative and influential, rather than an autocratic, leader. Towards this, he took courses in human psychology, attended executive training programs at IIM Bengaluru and, more importantly, sought feedback from people.

Seeing a reflection of his younger self in a lot of people around him who were technically sound, but needed support to move ahead, he took on the role of mentor and coach. He encouraged youngsters to focus not only on their technical but also on the softer skills, so crucial for career progression, and helped them structure their learning journeys. 'On one occasion, my entire team and I took a course offered by Indian Institute of Banking and Finance. And learning is contagious, as my boss was also influenced into resuming his learning journey!' he says. In a bid to engage with and encourage the youth, he started interacting with the student community in colleges, sharing his knowledge and helping them understand how to think differently.

Inculcate Cross Functional Skills

A financial services company was in the process of preparing a draft red herring prospectus (DRHP) in preparation for launching an initial public offering (IPO). A DRHP incorporates information about the company's business operations, financials, promoters, standing in the industry, plans for using the money and the risks that potential investors could run by investing in the company. Evidently, it is a comprehensive document wherein every statement has to be substantiated by relevant supporting documents with obvious legal and compliance implications.

The entire management team was pitching in the humungous task of preparing this very critical document. After contributing to the sections pertaining to their function, most department heads moved on, leaving the company secretary to anchor the rest of the process. But not Renuka, the forex department head. Out of her own interest and initiative, she worked along with the company secretary, actively co-ordinating with the merchant bankers, providing information, responding to queries, working with different departments to obtain the required documents, all done within very stringent timelines. She invested time in attending all the IPO-related meetings, learning along the way and contributing to discussions. She eventually became an integral part of the investor relations team.

The public relations and advertising activities kicked in soon after the DRHP had been filed and ratified by the regulator. Renuka again took it upon herself to work with the PR firm. She got her hands dirty ensuring the smooth turn out of all PR activities like the road shows and press conferences, taking complete ownership of the process.

What was her driver in investing time and energy into this initiative? She had not been tasked with this role. What was in it for her?

Renuka stood enriched by gaining a thorough knowledge of the IPO process, gaining visibility within the organization, building her network with prospective investors and making a place for herself as an integral member of the IPO team.

Enhance Your Degree

One of my former colleagues, working in the administration department of the organization, chose to pursue a management degree at Narsee Monjee Institute of Management Studies. Managing academics alongside a full-time job and home responsibilities entailed superhuman determination. What was her driving force in putting herself through this excruciatingly demanding schedule for three long years? 'I wanted to enhance my knowledge and stamp it with a recognized degree to give my career an impetus,' she said. Fast forward three years. Armed with a management degree, she sought a role change and was granted a position in the HR department. She grew to be a very successful professional and went on to build a thriving career in HR.

Another former colleague chose to pursue a master's degree in technology management at Columbia University, at a point when he was in the 18th year of a flourishing career in information technology (IT) at a Wall Street firm. What did he achieve by pursuing this degree at this stage in his career? 'This amazing journey encompassing both academic and experiential learning added different dimensions to my knowledge and perspective, provided an opportunity to engage with a diverse group of people and will, I hope, pave the way for more significant and elevated roles going forward,' he said.

So, fortify your intellectual capital with relevant degrees related to your domain and role.

Leverage Other Learning Opportunities

Write a Book

Writing a book is a tremendous learning experience as it entails a deep exploration of the subject by leveraging a spectrum of resources such as articles, books, discussions with practitioners and subject matter experts to garner their views, perspectives, subject knowledge, experiences and stories. This goes a long way in augmenting your own subject knowledge by adding different dimensions to it.

'Writing is an art of refining your own thinking. It is never about what you want to convey but what the reader understands,' says Abhijit Bhaduri, author of two bestselling books: The *Digital Tsunami* and *Don't Hire the Best—How to Hire for Culture Fit.* His upcoming book is *Dreamers & Unicorns—How Leadership, Talent and Culture Turn Dreamers into Unicorns.*

'Writing has helped me in consolidating and connecting my ideas and simplifying my thoughts so others can understand,' says Purna Chandra Rao Duggirala, or Chandoo, a teacher, trainer and an author of two books—*The Vlookup Book* and *The Dashboard for Excel* (co-authored with Jordan Goldmeier).

Madan Sabnavis, an economist and author of three books *Macro Economics Demystified, Eco-Quirks and Economics of India* and *Hits and Misses: The Indian Banking Story* says,

Writing a book is a journey undertaken on uncharted territory. While you start with a concrete subject, you cannot be sure as to how it will evolve as you move ahead. It entails drawing linkages with other subjects, past experiences and even movies, besides a deep dive analysis accomplished by referring to books, talking to and observing people, and through your own reasoning. Some of the explored concepts and topics may eventually not even feature in the book, but you stand enriched by having these firmly entrenched in your knowledge base. Writing a book is truly a tremendous learning experience.

Review a Book

Sabnavis has reviewed over 250 books on wide-ranging subjects such as management, politics, economics, religion as well as biographies, autobiographies and company profiles for various newspapers and magazines. This has gone a long way in broadening his knowledge base, complementing his own domain knowledge with several other dimensions; thus positioning him well to engage with people from different industries and professions in both serious discussions and small talk.

Being Imaginative

Your success is as much an outcome of your knowledge, skills and abilities as it is of your adeptness at questioning status quo and discerning potential problems and areas of improvement, and then leveraging your technical prowess to design novel solutions to address these. A strong brand is associated with adding value through creative solutions for enhancing efficiency or reducing cost. Consider these examples:

Film director Prasoon Pandey was struck with the idea of making a short film with a strong 'social distancing' message the day the COVID-19-prompted lockdown was announced. At his creative best, Pandey conceptualized a novel approach for shooting the film, without requiring anyone to move out of their homes. He initiated the project by getting his son to shoot a template of the film, wherein he played all the characters himself. Subsequently, the template was shared with the actors, so they could see how they were required to place themselves while shooting their assigned piece. The actors, Bollywood's creme de la creme, performed to perfection, taking cues from the template and getting a family member to shoot their piece. The individual frames were then pieced together with the director, editor and the music director working in unison. The film thus made, sans social contact, received a huge applause, with Pandey adding the tags of creativity and quick action to his brand.[1]

****

Nikhil Mariwala, a manager in the IT Function Transformation team at a global consulting firm, had just finished writing a client proposal when he sat down thinking, 'I can't be spending such insane hours writing just one proposal. The task is unquestionably complex, given the multifarious parameters that need to be factored in, but surely there is another, more efficient way of doing it?' Propelled by this thought and in consultation with his practice head, he set out to try his hand at designing a template for writing a proposal. Having thought it through, he came up with a template that could deliver proposals across service offerings and across industries in a fraction of the time it would normally take. Perceiving the obvious benefits of the template in terms of releasing hundreds of man hours, which could now be utilized in doing something more productive, it was quickly adopted by all the teams in his practice. With some periodic fine-tuning, the template is used even today. What did this mean for Mariwala? It not only eased his work and enhanced his productivity, it also catapulted him as a proposal-writing expert, adding a new area of expertise to this brand.

*****

The lockdown call in March 2020 had spelt doom for the annual sales strategy offsite that had been painstakingly planned at a manufacturing company. The team was resigned to postponing the event to a more opportune time. But not Raul! A senior sales manager, Raul was determined to make it happen as planned. Collaborating with his IT team, he explored various virtual meeting applications and conceptualized the format for the offsite. He presented a meticulous, skilfully devised, virtual offsite plan to the sales head the following morning, who was a bit cynical, initially, but finally gave his approval to go ahead.

The sales head set the context for the meeting to a 40-member strong sales team that had congregated in a virtual meeting room, with people joining from the comfort of their homes. After a brief discussion, the team was divided into four groups, each placed in a virtual break-out room. Each group was assigned a specific issue to brainstorm on. Subsequently, the four groups returned to the main room and presented their ideas, thoughts and plans to the larger group. The meeting was touted as highly successful, and Raul, who had no prior experience in facilitating a virtual meeting, was applauded for his creativity and resourcefulness. His brand stood enriched with descriptors like 'self-starter', 'go-getter' and 'willing to experiment'.

Being Far-sighted

Your success, whether in business or career management, requires the acumen to discern emerging market trends, with their concomitant opportunities and risks, and the boldness to recast your strategy to take advantage of opportunities and safeguard against the risks.

Getting Theatres Back to Action

The 1990s saw the decline of movie theatres with families choosing to watch movies on videos in the comfort of their living rooms, at a fraction of the cost of what it would take to go to the theatre. In wake of these changing viewer preferences, film distributers started releasing films simultaneously on video and in theatres. Theatres thus started falling to disuse, losing their sheen and heading towards rapid dilapidation.

Director Sooraj Barjatya[2] was instrumental in changing this trend through his audacious, game-changing strategy for distributing his film *Hum Aapke Hain Koun…!* He decided to release the film using the 'ultra stereo optical sound' technology to enable the audience to enjoy a superior audio-visual quality. Since most theatres did not have the infrastructure for this technology, he limited the release of the film to only those theatres that did, while pressing the others to acquire it. He also engaged with theatre owners, urging them to revamp their infrastructure in a bid to get them back in the game. Besides restricting the release of the film to a limited number of theatres, he also instituted strong safeguards against video piracy, besides delaying its release on video tapes.

His strategy proved to be a roaring success, as the film *Hum Aapke Hain Koun...!* became the biggest blockbuster and the highest grossing Indian film of the 1990s. It also heralded a turning point in the fortunes of theatres, which got back to action with families once again starting to make a beeline for theatres for a superior movie-watching experience. In resurrecting the big screen thus, Barjatya demonstrated immense far-sightedness, an astute understanding of consumer behaviour and a high degree of audaciousness in designing a marketing strategy to beat the current market trend.

The Birth of the Sachet

Back in the 1970s, shampoo was considered an upmarket product, meant only for the affluent, with limited availability only at stores that catered to the rich. Chinni Krishnan,[3] an agriculturist and a small-scale pharmaceutical packaging entrepreneur, stripped the shampoo off its elite tag with his groundbreaking invention—the sachet. He was driven by the belief that products enjoyed by the rich should also be within the reach of the common man at an affordable price. He started distributing products like salt and talcum powder, packaged in sachets, before adding other products to his list.

While the sachet was conceptualized and designed by Chinni Krishnan, the credit for posting it prominently in the repertoire of retail packaging goes to his son, C. K. Ranganathan. His company, CavinKare, launched its first product, Chik shampoo, with the sachet at the centre of its innovative distribution strategy. It made quick inroads into the untapped rural markets by making it possible even for the marginalized to buy shampoo, once touted as an elite product. Chik shampoo is the largest selling shampoo brand in several Indian states and continues to be CavinKare's flagship brand.

Chinni Krishnan's words that 'the sachet is the packaging product of the future' proved prophetic, as other FMCG giants were quick to adopt the sachet and leverage it as their preferred packaging product to tap into the erstwhile untouched rural market.

Scooters to Power Bikes

People were dismayed when Bajaj Auto's Managing Director, Rajiv Bajaj, made the bold decision in 2009 to bring down the curtains on its flagship product—the scooter, which had been popularly known as 'Hamara Bajaj—the nation's family car on two wheels' for decades. He was astute in discerning the changing preferences of the consumer and their emerging proclivity for motorcycles, and in responding to it with a decision to make a foray into the motorcycle market. He sought to position Bajaj Auto as a motorcycle specialist, with a clear and sharp focus on the global motorcycle market. He forged partnerships with global motorcycle majors such as KTM, Triumph and Husqvarna for taking his strategy forward. The strategy bore fruit as it helped resurrect the struggling fortunes of the company.[4]

In 2019, he chose to re-enter the scooter market in wake of the newly found consumer preference for gearless scooters and the subsequent growth in the sector. He re-introduced the iconic Chetak scooter in its gearless avatar.

Sooraj Barjatya, Chinni Krishnan and Rajiv Bajaj demonstrated immense astuteness in perceiving the changes in consumer preferences and market trends and immense audaciousness in recasting their business strategies to take advantage of the changing market dynamics. Their game-changing strategies enhanced their brands with the labels of 'business acumen' and 'strategist'.

Strategizing Your Career

Take a page from the stories of Sooraj Barjatya, Chinni Krishnan and Rajiv Bajaj for strategizing your own career and building a supporting brand.

It would be prudent, in this context, to be conscious of the going trends in your company, industry and domain and manoeuvre your career to leverage the opportunities and safeguard against the threats that these trends represent. Given below are a few general 2020 industry trends.

1. Emerging, new-age technologies like artificial intelligence, machine learning, design thinking, robotic process automation, digital marketing and natural language processing present tremendous opportunities.

2. With machines being programmed to achieve increasingly complex tasks, automation and its concomitant robots and bots pose a serious threat to a wide range of jobs across sectors.

3. Permanent jobs are making way for short-term contractual jobs or freelance work.

4. Data analytics is the going buzzword, making inroads into every industry and every function, with the tall promise of rendering decisions faster, sharper and more effective.

5. Edu-tech, health-tech, fin-tech, digital marketing and gaming are the promising, high-growth sectors.

In addition to these broad trends, think of the specific developments in your own space.

1. What are the current trends in your company?

2. Which direction is your industry moving towards?

3. What are the emerging roles in your domain? Which roles are on the decline?

CALL FOR ACTION

Strategizing Your Career

1. In the table below, mark the knowledge, skills and capabilities that are:

   • Relevant for succeeding in your current role,

   • Needed to prepare for your aspired role,

   • Needed in the context of the opportunities presented by the current industry trends,

   • Needed in the context of the threats presented by the current industry trends.

Feel free to add to the list of competencies given in the table.

2. Rate your current and desired levels of competence on the relevant elements in the list on a 5-point scale, where 1 = low and 5 = high.

3. Identify the timelines for achieving this.

S. N.	Elements	Current Role		Aspired Role		Timelines
		Current Rating	Desired Rating	Current Rating	Desired Rating	
1	Communication skills					
2	Presentation skills					
3	People management					
4	Team management					
5	Networking skills					
6	Time management and prioritization					
7	Industry knowledge					
8	Business knowledge					
9	Regulatory knowledge					
10	Other					

4. What strategic moves can revitalize your career? Think through the following.

- How long have you been in your current role? Do you get a sense that you have outgrown it?

- What are the other allied roles that you may want to explore?

- Would it be judicious to explore alternative roles in your own company, other companies in the same industry or in one of the emerging industries?

- Would it be more enriching and judicious to transition from a full time to a contractual, assignment-based work format, or vice versa?

1. Substance, the mainstay of your brand, embodies your reliability, trustworthiness and authenticity. It emanates from your propensity to act ethically and your ability to deliver business results based on your professional competence.

2. Your professional competence is the sum of your knowledge, skills, qualification, experience and track record and the way you demonstrate it in different work scenarios.

3. It would be judicious to proactively adjust your brand by incorporating the relevant skills, in the wake of the going industry trends and their likely impact on your career.

4. It would be prudent to inculcate the qualities of being:

a. **A Constant Learner**

    i. There is truth in Albert Einstein's astute observation, 'The day you stop learning, is the day you start dying. It is critical to inculcate learning, touted as the master of all skills.

    ii. Conduct an audit of your knowledge, skills and abilities in the context of industry trends and your current and aspired roles; identify gaps, if any, and design an action plan for bridging them.

b. **Imaginative**

    i. Inculcate the mindset of being curious, questioning the status quo and identifying opportunities for engendering efficiency and reducing cost; thus relating your brand with creativity, resourcefulness and out-of-box thinking.

c. **Far-sighted**

    i. It is important to inculcate the acumen for discerning industry trends, spotting opportunities and threats and recasting your career strategy in response to these observations and insights.

References

1. New Indian Express [Internet]. Came up with the idea when COVID-19 lockdown was announced: Prasoon Pandey on short film 'Family'. 8 April 2020. Available from: https://www.newindianexpress.com/entertainment/hindi/2020/apr/08/came-up-with-the-idea-when-covid-19-lockdown-was-announced-prasoon-pandey-on-short-film-family-2127437.html

2. DailyHunt [Internet]. 25 years of Hum Aapke Hain Koun: how a film rejected by the trade created history. Mon, Aug 5. Available from: https://m.dailyhunt.in/news/nepal/english/cinestaan-epaper-cinestan/25+years+of+hum+aapke+hain+koun+how+a+film+rejected+by+the+trade+created+history-newsid-129007116

3. India Today [Internet]. The right package. 31 Dec 2007. Available from: https://www.indiatoday.in/magazine/cover-story/story/20071231-the-right-package-734855-2007-12-20

4. Economic Times [Internet]. Bajaj to stop scooter production, focus on motorcycles. 10 Dec 2009. Available from: https://economictimes.indiatimes.com/bajaj-to-stop-scooter-production-focus-on-motorcycles/articleshow/5320461.cms?from=mdr

03

Connect

The Second Dimension

Chapter 5

The Power of a Network

In its quest to enhance the productivity of its engineers and scientists, Bell Labs[1] had engaged Robert Kelley and Janet Caplan, authors of the Harvard Business Review article 'How Bell Labs Creates Star Performers', to understand what differentiated their star performers, comprising 10–15 per cent of their workforce, from the rest, who were 'simply good, solid middle performers'. Considering that the work turned out of Bell Labs has been the recipient of nine Nobel prizes, clearly anyone getting through its doors must have a superlative intelligence quotient. This was corroborated by Kelley and Caplan's research which found that the key differentiators between the star and the middle-ranking performers lay not in their cognitive skills but in their work strategies.

They identified nine such work strategies which contributed to the superior performance of stars at Bell Labs. The top two of these were—*taking initiative* and *networking*. The authors stated in the article that when faced with a technical issue,

An average performer painstakingly called various technical gurus and then waited, wasting valuable time, while calls went unreturned and e-mail messages unanswered. Star performers, however, rarely face such situations because they do the work of building reliable networks before they actually need them. When they call someone for advice, stars almost always get a faster answer.

Clearly, relationships act as social lubricants to elicit faster responses from stakeholders leading to higher productivity and greater success.

The power of a network in reinforcing your brand by enhancing your productivity, in addition to facilitating access to opportunities for your professional and personal advancement, strengthening your wellbeing and general quality of life, is unquestionable.

Each one of us has developed a network of social connections during the course of life. This network has probably evolved by chance without much thought and effort. We tend to forge relationships, for instance, with colleagues whom we are dependent on for turning in our deliverables. Then there are industry colleagues, former colleagues, people we meet at conferences, training programs and seminars, those we travel with or share common interests with—members of yoga, trekking and cycling clubs—and those of other social entities like housing societies and community groups, along with neighbours, friends and family. Very loosely stated, this comprises our network.

Tian Zheng,[2] a professor in the department of statistics at Columbia University, led a study in 2009 to understand how many people are known to an average person. Based on a set of questions administered to 1,500 people in the USA, the study found that, on an average, a person knows about 600 people. Given that we also have indirect access to the networks of people we are directly connected with, our network has the potential to grow exponentially. Do the math—multiply 600 by 600—the figure thrown up is astronomical! 'Your network is your net worth,' says Porter Gale,[3] the author of *Your Network Is Your Net Worth*. *But is this network really your net worth or your social capital?*

This large, unwieldy, impersonal network may or may not serve you well for meeting your goals and aspirations; because what you need, in fact, is a more focused, meaningful and enduring set of relationships. In an interview published in a 2013 *Forbes*[4] article titled 'Worth More Than Money', Gale said,

I don't believe it's the size of the network that is important. I believe it is the quality of the relationships and your ability to make authentic connections that most greatly impact your true worth. I believe that seeking out and working in collaboration with others who share your interests and values will provide a stronger foundation, enabling you to reach a higher level of success than you would on your own.

Consider the case study given below.

Vishesh was the HR business partner for three of the largest verticals at the India office of a global investment bank. His constituency comprised a little over 2,000 people, with the four delivery heads being his focal points of contact. Recognized for his functional prowess, Vishesh leveraged an effective tracking system that he had developed, to always be on top of things, ensuring a smooth and timely implementation of all the HR processes in his constituency. He invested time every week to engage with employees, both formally and informally, proactively understanding and resolving their grievances. He shared timely updates with the four delivery heads regularly, meeting them for lunch occasionally and playing table tennis with them after office hours, thus forging an excellent relationship.

Vishesh also set up regular fortnightly meetings with his boss, Snigdha, the HR head, proactively keeping her in loop of things. He was known to be her blue-eyed boy because of his successful engagement with his constituency. He often had lunch with his colleagues Sheena, Rahul and Roshini, the other HR business partners, who were pretty senior in the team, and also kept in touch with his counterparts at other locations on phone and email. He was abreast of the organizational developments as a result of his interaction with people in different parts of the organization. He had built a strong and empowered team, especially his two team leads, whom he had effectively delegated work to. This was one of the reasons he was able to make time to connect and build relationships with his wider ecosystem, which always stood him and his team in good stead.

Vishesh never missed an opportunity to attend HR conferences and other external forums where he got to meet his industry colleagues. These engagements kept him abreast of industry trends and helped him gather market intelligence when needed. He was particularly engaged with his counterparts in five other investment banks, taking turns with them to host HR discussion circles. On one occasion, when Snigdha was unable to make it for a speaking engagement at an external forum, on account of a personal exigency, it was Vishesh whom she had passed the baton to. In fact, Vishesh was called upon to step in for Snigdha whenever she went on leave and was touted as a strong contender for a promotion that year.

His colleague, Sheena, the other HR business partner, was very hands-on with all HR activities, preferring to do things herself, with the result she ended up spending almost 90 per cent of her time with the employees. She was popular in her constituency and was often lauded for her work by the delivery heads, as she was available for the employees and worked hard towards resolving their issues. But apart from meeting Vishesh, Rahul and Roshini, she was not particularly plugged into the rest of the HR team. Her interaction with her other HR colleagues was limited, as she was hardly ever around, preferring to spend most of her time with her constituency which operated from a different location. So engrossed was Sheena with her clients that she often slipped on her meetings with the HR head. As a result, Sheena did not get the extent of support that she needed from Snigdha and other HR colleagues, as Vishesh did.

Rahul was always reluctant to move out of office, seldom making it to external industry events. While his internal network was strong, he knew very few people outside the organization. Therefore, he always fell short when he was called upon to gather market intelligence on HR matters, and a few months down the line, when he was seeking alternate employment, he had no industry contacts to turn to, barring a few placement consultants.

Roshini, on the other hand, was extremely engaged with the broader HR team as well as the employees in her constituency but did not invest time connecting with the delivery heads to understand their needs and build rapport. She was undoubtedly doing good work, but since they were not always in the know of things, they were not inclined to give her the feedback that she deserved.

So, what differentiated Vishesh from his colleagues Rahul, Sheena and Roshini? What contributed to his stellar performance?

Undoubtedly, all the four were well equipped with the requisite domain knowledge and functional proficiency to succeed in their roles. But one striking factor that distinguished Vishesh from the others was his robust network—the web of relationships he had forged with his business partners, team and boss internally and with his industry peers externally. Leveraging his excellent interpersonal and people management skills, he had adopted a conscious, deliberate and strategic approach towards connecting with people and building an effective network, which served him well and was instrumental in his success.

The effectiveness of Rahul, Sheena and Roshini, on the other hand, was somewhat diminished because of their failure to build a well-rounded network. Sheena, for instance, was completely focused on her constituency, overlooking other important stakeholders like the broader HR team and the HR head, whose support was critical for her success. Rahul, on the other hand, had worked on building good connections internally within the organization but had not forged any connections externally. And Roshini failed to build bridges with her most important stakeholders—the delivery heads.

A supportive ecosystem, comprising a network of relationships, that can be leveraged for eliciting a timely response to queries, access to organizational information, assistance in negotiating through the organization's political dynamics and obtaining support for one's emotional well-being is, thus, critical for success. It is even more important to build and nurture a network, as you move ahead in your career and your operational turf expands in terms of the number of players and the complexity of the tasks and relationships that you are called upon to manage. By enhancing your impact and influence, a robust network strengthens the power of your brand.

Build Three Types of Networks

What is the ideal shape and size of your network?

The answer to this question depends largely on what your goals are and what you are striving for. Since cultivating a network requires

Figure 5.1. Three Networks

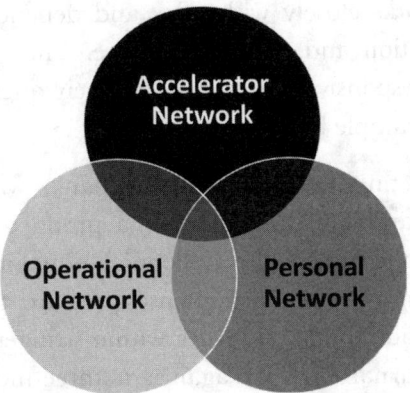

an investment of time and energy, you need to think strategically and focus on developing broadly three types of networks.

1. Operational Network
2. Personal Network
3. Accelerator Network

Operational Network

Your operational network is pre-defined by your role vis-à-vis the organizational structure. It comprises people whom you are dependent on for turning out your daily deliverables. For instance, a project manager in a manufacturing set-up is inherently connected with people in the design, shop floor, procurement and marketing departments, besides the client and senior management. A salesperson in an insurance company is required to interface with the marketing, operations and the product teams to service clients and their success in closing deals depends partly on the cooperation and support of colleagues in these departments. As an example, an executive in operations may support a salesperson by expediting the process towards the end of the month to help them hit their monthly target. Similarly, the accounts receivable department works closely with sales and depends on them for payment collection and accounts closure. Their success hinges partly on the responsiveness of sales to their queries and needs. Consider the example below.

Neha, a marketing professional in a bank, was tasked with launching a marketing campaign for a product that had been developed specifically for the millennial population. Since the marketing team was under immense pressure to generate an immediate impact, she had to work within stringent timelines—a mere 30-day turnaround, as against a three-month lead time normally estimated for a campaign like this.

The project entailed getting multiple teams to the table, each with varying degrees of motivation and interest in the project. She sprang into action, getting the teams on board and garnering their support through her inclusive and collaborative approach. She got the campaign on its feet within a record 29 days, receiving a big applause from her stakeholders.

Debriefing with me on this project later, Neha attributed her success to the enthusiastic cooperation of people, which was largely a fall out of the strong relationships she had forged with other teams. People responded to her calls faster and more willingly because of the personal rapport that she shared with them.

Similarly, at various points of my career, it was partly my personal rapport with project managers and department heads that helped me garner their support in designing and rolling out various HR policies, events and processes successfully.

Personal Network

This network provides personal support and energy and is, therefore, vital for facilitating balance and harmony in life. It comprises people who help address your emotional needs—someone you can vent out to on a bad day, turn to for empathy and advice and discuss a difficult situation with, without the fear of being judged. This is a network you can engage with to pursue common interests, people with whom you can take a walk or play a game of cricket or cards, unwind over a cup of coffee or go to the movies.

Close to four decades ago, like many other students in Dehradun, I was striving to pursue my graduation at Delhi University. I had made it to the first admission list of a prestigious college, based on my decent grades. Anticipating the admission process to be a cake walk, therefore, I set out for Delhi with my father with a spring in my step and a song in my heart. I sailed through the interview, where I got to meet the principal and some of the professors, and much to my delight, I was asked to proceed to the admission office to complete the admission formalities.

I stood in the queue eagerly waiting for my turn, and when the admission officer laid out the list of documents to be submitted, I pulled out each document from my folder with a flourish of an athlete running the victory lap. But the very next moment, my heart sank and my head started to spin, when it dawned on me that one of the crucial documents that was required to seal the admission was missing. I stood there, not knowing quite what to do.

After dealing with my father's wrath at my carelessness, I put on my thinking cap to figure out ways to salvage the situation. I remember being told that the principal of the college had a sister-in-law who lived in Dehradun, and that she was a friend of a friend of my parents, reminiscent of *six degrees of separation*,[5] an idea propounded by the American social psychologist Stanley Milgram in 1967, to indicate that each person is six or less social connections away from any other person on the planet. Going by this theory, I realized that the principal was only four social connections away from me!

Armed with this data point, and determined to resurrect the situation, I accosted the principal, whom I saw sprinting across to the other college building and explained the situation. I requested her to grant me one day to make a quick trip to Dehradun and collect the missing document from school. But she would hear none of it. 'There is a kilometer long list of students awaiting a call from this college,' she said. As a last-ditch attempt, at that stage I told her that her sister-in-law, who lived in Dehradun, was known to my parents through a friend and once again pleaded my case. Much to my delight, this time she relented! My breath eased, and finally securing the admission after submitting the missing document the following day, I heaved a big sigh of relief. The power of a network dawned on me at that moment!

Similarly, a friend who was undergoing a bad patch in personal life found solace in her college alumni group with whom she started engaging socially, turning to for advice and even taking holidays with.

I am a part of a yoga group, a trekking group and a walking group from which I derive immense energy and a sense of well-being. A group of ladies has formed a laughing club in our housing society. They meet every single morning, come rain, hail or storm, promoting fitness and positive thinking and deriving energy from each other. During my morning walks, I often overhear them discussing personal issues and offering each other empathy and advice.

My father is a part of a coffee club, and barring Sundays, they engage in small talk and exchange news over coffee at 12 noon every day. They derive joy through birthday celebrations and are there for each other in moments of crisis.

Just as in personal life, one requires personal connections at the workplace, someone to talk to and pursue extra-curricular interests and enjoy camaraderie and warmth with.

Accelerator Network

An accelerator network comprises people who will advocate you, mentor you, advise you, coach you, support your learning and point you to potential opportunities and threats. A salesperson, for instance, may receive referrals from their manager, valuable insights on the art of persuasive selling from a mentor and a heads-up about a potential vacancy at another location from a colleague, which would enable the salesperson to pitch for a coveted role, about which they may not have otherwise known. This would go a long way in supporting their career progression. Let's explore this further.

Sponsors: The Influential Advocates

Sheryl Sandberg, the chief operating officer (COO) of Facebook, who figured in the *Time 100* annual list of the most influential people in the world in 2012, besides regularly showing up on the *Fortune 50* most powerful women list, acknowledged Larry Summers' support, advocacy and mentorship in a Harvard Business Review interview[6] saying, 'I have had a lot of mentors over the course of my career, Larry being one of the absolutely most important and certainly the first.'

She first met Larry Summers when she was studying economics at Harvard in 1987. She wrote in a 2008 article,

A friend and I were forming a new student organization, Women in Economics and Government, to encourage women to major in these subjects. We told all of our professors of our efforts and of all of them, the one who helped us the most was Larry. He served as our champion and helped rally the support of his fellow professors behind our efforts.

Sheryl Sandberg, Larry Summers' True Record on Women. HuffPost [Internet]. 12/8/2008 Available from: https://www.huffpost.com/entry/what-larry-summers-has-do_b_142126

'The following year, when I wanted to write my senior thesis on the economics of spousal abuse, Larry volunteered to be my advisor,' she said in the same article.

When Larry Summers became the chief economist at the World Bank in 1991, he recruited Sandberg as his research assistant where she worked for about a year on health projects in India. Subsequently, when he moved to serve as the United States secretary of the treasury under President Bill Clinton, he once again enlisted Sandberg as his chief of staff to assist in the treasury's work on debt relief in the developing world during the Asian financial crisis. She later joined Google and went on to gain unprecedented fame in the world of technology. 'And those opportunities are ones I wouldn't have had without him,' says Sandberg.

A sponsor, therefore, has the currency, connections and power to speak for you and endorse you when you are not in the room, by providing objective examples of your capability during critical discussions regarding promotions, performance appraisal and allocation of career enhancing assignments.[6] According to Sylvia Ann Hewlett, the founding president of Center for Work-Life Policy, a New York based think tank that designs policies for enhancing work-life balance, a sponsor can confer a statistical career benefit of 22–30 per cent on a protégé.

Mentorship: A Mentor Empowers You

By sharing experiences and perspective, providing insights on navigating through the organizational dynamics, offering feedback and lending visibility via introduction to a wider network of people, the role of a mentor in a person's career growth is undoubtedly important. Consider the following examples.

One of my bosses, who also doubled up as a mentor and friend, would always listen to my rants with empathy, but never hesitated to offer candid feedback identifying elements in my work and behaviour that could be mitigating my effectiveness. I remember, she had walked up to my work area once and pointed at all the little things on my desk that had outlived their usefulness, such as pens that had run out of ink, visiting cards that were outdated and documents pinned on my soft board that were obsolete. 'To be a role model for your team, it is not enough to be good at what you do. Appearance matters too. And appearance is not just about what you wear, but also about how you keep your desk and anything else that people can observe and draw impressions from,' she had explained. She had, in fact, given me my first lesson in personal branding!

*****

To this day, Anirudh, a marketing manager at an insurance company, is grateful to a senior consultant in his company who was instrumental in pushing him to polish his presentation skills and grooming him for stellar performances at the marketing review meetings. 'Since she had been in the company far longer than I had, she knew my stakeholders very well in terms of what would resonate with them, based on their current priorities and concerns, and therefore their expectations from these reviews. Her guidance on points to be highlighted and the ones to be understated was indeed very valuable. Besides grilling me on the content over several iterations, she would compel me to rehearse the presentation several times over till I would know it from the back of my hand. This enabled me to go in confidently and emerge with flying colours in these meetings. I am thankful to her for investing time tutoring me and facilitating my personal development,' he says.

Relationships Matter: Knowing the Right People

Knowing the right people can open doors and provide opportunity. All other things being equal, an interviewer is likely to select the person they know, have interacted with and have a positive impression about, compared to the one whom they are meeting for the first time. Studies show that for every one hour that a well-networked employee awaits a response, the average waits three to five hours. Relationships matter!

Sarvesh Kumar joined a multinational accounting and consulting firm as senior director after a successful stint with an education start-up, which he had co-founded with a friend. A year into his new role, he had the opportunity to represent his group at a week-long, mega funding event run by the firm. This annual event provided a platform for different business units, which tended to work almost as independent organizations, to compete for budget allocation by presenting and pitching their vision for the coming year.

A jury would then select the best ideas worthy of the firm's investment. The jury comprised a cross functional core team of senior executives as well as representatives of the participating business units, who were called upon to rate all the entries, barring the one submitted by their own business unit. The participating teams were free to socialize with the jury members to communicate and clarify the merit of their ideas. They could meet them informally on and off campus in order to get them interested in their idea and garner their support.

The biggest challenge, however, was to set up these informal touch points, given that all the teams were competing hard for obtaining face time with jury members within very stringent timelines. In such a scenario, a strong network was a huge advantage as people would respond more readily and swiftly to the calls of those whom they knew well. They were also more likely to listen to them with a more open mind and with a greater degree of receptivity to their ideas.

Sarvesh and his team of four were well placed in this respect as between them they were connected well with almost all the jury members. Therefore, not only did they find it easier to set up these meetings, the jury members also tended to have more detailed interactions with them as a result of these relationships. In one such interaction, Sarvesh and his team learnt that ideas based on a broader perspective and those with a greater potential to impact the firm at a macro level were likely to be viewed more favourably by the jury. As an immediate response, they added another layer to their presentation changing its orientation from an inward group focus to a broader organizational focus. Needless to say that they won the contest!

Referrals Open New Doors

A study by Lou Adler,[7] author and CEO, Performance-based Hiring Learning Systems, found that networking trumped all other means of finding new jobs, for both active as well as casual job seekers. Similarly, the role of personal contacts in growing a business is also well known.

I experienced this first-hand when I shifted gears to move from a regular corporate job to a consulting role in 2012. Since then, I have had the opportunity to engage with more than 55 organizations across six industries. I have reached out to approximately 500 companies to have landed with assignments with 55, assuming a hit rate of 10 per cent. Never a fan of cold calling, I have relied mainly on my direct contacts and on those in their networks to facilitate introductions to potential clients. My experience aligns with the American sociologist Professor Mark Granovetter's theory, promulgated in his seminal article 'The Strength of Weak Ties', where he established that within a social network, it is the weak or the indirect, rather than the strong or the direct ties that are more powerful in pointing to opportunities.

I have been referred to companies by my family, friends, former colleagues, neighbours and, more importantly, people in their networks. For instance, my neighbour who works for a multinational accounting firm introduced me to the talent head, paving the way for my association with the firm a few years later. Another acquaintance, the CEO of an insurance company, referred me to his company's HR team, thus facilitating my partnership with that company. Two former colleagues whom I was still connected with had forwarded my marketing material to the talent management teams in their respective organizations, thus making way for my partnerships with two global banks. A friend's husband, who is the COO of a pharmaceutical company, regularly sends his team for my open workshops.

Similarly, while out on a trek with a trekking and cycling group, I had the opportunity of presenting my work to a bunch of professionals with a backdrop of the gentle breeze rustling the wide-ranging trees on the hillside. On one such trek, I met the HR executive of one of the Larsen & Toubro group companies, which landed me my first assignment with the company a few months later. Similarly, I met a senior manager from Mahindra & Mahindra on another trek, who sent a couple of people to one of my open workshops a year later.

Not all the referrals translated into business, of course, but they did present an opportunity by opening up that critical first door for a conversation which, to my mind, is the toughest. Subsequently, what you do with the opportunity really depends on your expertise, credibility and client-handling skills.

Knowledge and Insights

Working as a solo consultant, I felt very isolated during the COVID-19-induced lockdown initially. But gradually, I took the initiative to reach out to people and in the ensuing conversations got to hear about the varied experiences of people in different industries, from the travails of working from home to the impact of the economic downturn and dwindling cash flows, trends in HR, jobs rendered redundant, the hot and upcoming skills, efficacy of virtual training and proclivity of people towards adopting it. I stood enriched from these insights and realized that the wider your network of informed contacts, the greater your access to new and valuable information.

Similarly, when writing articles and designing new training programs, in addition to my own research, I follow the practice of connecting with people to bounce off ideas and gather new perspectives. I have found that people are forthcoming, willingly sharing their stories and experiences. Some have even introduced me to people in their networks for further interaction and engagement. By adding new dimensions to my knowledge, these informal conversations form an important means for augmenting my learning and development.

Getting Right Information at Right Time

One of my senior stakeholders, whom I occasionally met for coffee, once gave me a heads-up about a potential threat to my role during one of our coffee meetings. He sounded me off about some adverse comments that had been made about my team in one of the management meetings when I was not present. His word of caution galvanized me to action. I delved into the issue, met up with the concerned stakeholders, clarified things and swiftly took the necessary corrective actions. This senior stakeholder stood right behind me, fully supportive of this damage-control exercise. I was able to prevent a relatively minor issue from snowballing into something more serious, as a result of the early word of caution I had received during our informal interaction.

How does information flow in an organization?

Formal Communication Channels

Information flows through formal channels like town halls, meetings, emails, websites, the media, as well as informal channels, better known as grapevine or water-cooler conversations. Needless to say that the information published on formal channels is totally authentic, since it comes from the most trusted organizational sources. Therefore, its usefulness in understanding and keeping abreast of the events and other developments in the organization is indisputable. This information, however, is slow to travel, as it is authenticated at multiple check points along the way, before it is eventually reported. By the time it reaches you, it might be too late for you to leverage it to your advantage, since events, people and situations might have long been churning around behind the scenes. Reena's story is a case in point.

Reena works as an operations manager at the Mumbai office of a global bank. At a recent departmental meeting, she was taken by surprise when it was announced that a particular banking process, which was currently being run out of Australia for all the bank's entities across the globe, would be transitioned to India over the next few months, and her colleague, Rahul, would be taking the lead for migrating the process. In fact, he was slated to travel to Australia later that month to meet his counterparts to facilitate knowledge transfer and work out a transition plan. Reena's face fell when she heard this, since she had not only been working on a very similar process but also had prior experience on a migration project. She, therefore, considered herself much better qualified for leading a project such as this. She grumbled and fretted thinking how unfair the world was.

Reena may have lost out on multiple counts, but a glaring point that stands out is that she had no idea that this transition was in the offing. In fact, she learnt about it when it was announced during the departmental meeting at a point when Rahul had already been identified for leading the project. Had she been in the know early enough, she could have pitched for the role at the very least. But the way things played out, she was not even a contender in the game.

How come this important piece of information had given Reena a miss? Perhaps she was not plugged into the bank's grapevine.

Grapevine: The Informal Communication Channels

Beneath the layer of the formal network defined by the organizational structure lies an informal network of people that transcends these formal reporting lines. The informal communication channels, or grapevine, that criss-cross this informal network run far ahead of the official communication channels. Grapevine gives you access to information early enough, to enable you to deal with people, situations and events proactively, while they are still in motion. It allows you to stay ahead of decisions that can impact you, your career and your team.

Grapevine keeps you in the know of informal and seemingly unimportant office banter like the reason for the CEO's visit to a particular location, outcome of the recently held management team offsite, people who are currently in favour and those who are not, person poised for that next big role, businesses on an expansion spree and those on the decline. These random data points give you a sense of the organizational environment and allow you to spot opportunities that you could take advantage of, and threats that you could proactively defend yourself against.

People often question the authenticity of information delivered on grapevine. I have posed this question to thousands of people and most often the responses are laced with 'ifs' and 'buts' and 'depends who it is coming from', or 'how trustworthy the person is'. In my experience, just about 20 per cent people really acknowledge the importance of being plugged into grapevine, while the rest of the majority think of it as a time-wasting activity, akin to rumour-mongering gossip, something they prefer not to be seen engaging in. Interestingly, Keith Davis[8] in his classic study on grapevine found 'that in normal business situations between

75% and 95% of grapevine information is correct'. Grapevine, therefore, constitutes a very important source of information that you would ignore at your own peril.

Seema, one of my team members, was very keen to move from her current role in learning and development to one in recruitment. She was looking for an exposure to different HR verticals to prepare for a more rounded, senior-level role in HR in the next few years. She had been scouting around for a recruitment role for some time, but it had not clicked so far. Soon thereafter, I happened to learn from a friend in a competing organization that one of our recruitment folks had shown up for an interview in his office the previous week, which meant that this person was actively exploring the job market and was bound to move out sooner rather later. Acting on this information, I started advocating Seema for a recruitment role to our stakeholders. I got her involved in one of the weekend recruitment drives to enable her to showcase her skills and gain visibility. As expected, this person soon put in her papers which paved the way for Seema's movement into that role.

I was able to facilitate Seema's movement because I got to know about the recruitment executive's impending movement ahead of my peers, which clearly gave me a clear advantage over the other contenders when pitching for the role. Such is the power of information, more specifically, timely information. Being in the know is, undoubtedly, an indispensable career skill.

How Does Grapevine Work?

According to the corporate anthropologist and social network analysis pioneer[8] Dr Karen Stephenson, three important roles form the cornerstone of informal networks that keep the grapevine running and thriving—the hubs, the gatekeepers and the pulse takers.

- *The hubs*

  Friendly and outgoing, the hubs are connected with people across the length and breadth of the organization. Socially adept, they are often found chatting at the water cooler or stopping by to say hello, picking up information as they move along engaging with people. The hubs, therefore, tend to learn about the latest organizational happenings ahead of anyone else. Quick as they are in gathering information, they are just as quick in dispensing it. If a word needs to be disseminated to people at the grassroots, it is enough to let the word out to the hubs and they can be trusted to do the rest. Considered valuable, people tend to look up to the hubs.

- *The gatekeepers*

  The gatekeepers hold the keys to the informal communication channels that run across functions, departments and locations. They broker information between the informal networks in different parts of the organization by either facilitating or impeding the communication channels.

- *The pulse takers*

  The pulse takers can read the pulse of the organization and have maximum indirect ties. They are described by Dr Stephenson as 'unseen but all seeing.' They wield a lot of clout that tends to be subtle and beneath the surface.

There is obviously an overlap between these roles, as people could be playing multiple roles in this fascinating world of informal information transmission.

Engaging on Grapevine

How do you get on the bandwagon of the grapevine?

First, acknowledge the importance of being in the know. Instead of keeping your nose to the grindstone through the day and looking upon water-cooler banter as a time waster, understand its importance and develop a mindset for engaging with people. Then unplug your headphones and connect with people informally to plug into the grapevine. Engage with people over lunch and coffee, during smoke breaks and while travelling to and from office.

Second, rather than sticking with a few friends, enlarge the group of people you interact with. Instead of having lunch with the same group day in and day out, keep aside a couple days every week to meet up with a different group. Expand your circle.

Third, identify the hubs, gatekeepers and pulse takers and seek opportunities to connect with them.

Fourth, remember that information comes at a premium. People disclose and trade information with those they like and trust and those who can reciprocate by feeding them information in turn. So stay tuned, and be a dispenser of information occasionally for people to consider you attractive and valuable.

Fifth, grapevine conversations can easily degenerate into negative gossip. Be judicious in differentiating between the useful and the negative. Keep away from the negative as it would not reflect well on you.

Sixth, assess the people you are talking to and trading information with. Make sure that they are trustworthy.

CALL FOR ACTION

Introspection: Are You in the Know?

- Do you hear about organizational information ahead of its dissemination through formal channels like town halls, meetings, emails and websites?

- Who are the hubs, people known to be 'in the know' in your organization?

- Are you connected with them?

- Identify the steps you can take to be better plugged into the grapevine.

PERSONAL BRANDING TIPS

- A robust network augments the power of your brand by enhancing your productivity, providing opportunities for career advancement and supporting your well-being.

- While the composition of your network depends on your goals, a well-rounded web of relationships broadly comprises three networks:

  o *An operational network* comprising people whose support is imperative for turning out your day-to-day deliverables.

  o *A personal network* encompassing relationships that provide personal support and energy, thus facilitating balance and harmony in life.

  o *An accelerator network* covering people who advocate you, provide advice and perspective, offer opportunities to learn and develop and help you remain abreast of organizational information.

- These networks could be overlapping.

- The authenticity of information flowing through the grapevine is considered to be in the north of 75 per cent. By providing information ahead of the official channels, grapevine positions you well in turning impending situations to your advantage.

- By not engaging on the grapevine, you may be left on the outside looking in.

References

1. Kelley R, Caplan J. How Bell Labs creates star performers. Harv Bus Rev [Internet]. July–Aug 1993.Available from: https://hbr.org/1993/07/how-bell-labs-creates-star-performers

2. Gelman A. The average American knows how many people? The New York Times [Internet]. 18 Feb 2013. Available from: https://www.nytimes.com/2013/02/19/science/the-average-american-knows-how-many-people.html

3. Gale P. Your network is your net worth: unlock the hidden power of connections for wealth, success, and happiness in the digital age. New York: Simon & Schuster; 2013.

4. Schawbel D. Porter Gale: why your connections are worth more than money. Forbes [Internet]. 4 Jun 2013. Available from: https://www.forbes.com/sites/danschawbel/2013/06/04/porter-gale/?sh=5a6dc658155b

5. Psychology Today [Internet]. Six degrees of separation: two new studies test 'six degrees of separation' hypothesis. 1 November 2003. Available from: https://www.psychologytoday.com/intl/articles/200311/six-degrees-separation

6. Harvard Business Review [Internet]. Sheryl Sandberg: the HBR interview. 2013. Available from: https://hbr.org/podcast/2013/03/sheryl-sandberg-the-hbr-interview

7. Adler L. New survey reveals 85% of all jobs are filled via networking. LinkedIn Pulse [Internet]. 29 Feb 2016. Available from: https://www.linkedin.com/pulse/new-survey-reveals-85-all-jobs-filled-via-networking-lou-adler/

8. Mishra J. Managing the grapevine. SAGE Publications [Internet]. 1 June 1990. Available from: https://journals.sagepub.com/doi/10.1177/009102609001900209

Chapter 6

Your Networking Plan

Serendipitous Networking

I was at the Narsee Monjee Institute of Management Studies campus in Mumbai to attend a talk on a hot Sunday afternoon in 2005. I stepped out after the talk in a rush to get back to run my Sunday errands. But as an afterthought, deciding to stay on a bit longer, I got talking to a group people. A quick introductory round gave us a sense of each other's professions, roles and organizations. During the course of the conversation, one person in the group mentioned that she had recently interviewed at Capgemini, which hadn't worked out for her, and offered to share the details of the open position with whoever was interested in applying. Obtaining the details from her, I called the person the following day, was invited for an interview a day later and landed with an appointment letter a week thereafter. My tryst with Capgemini was, thus, the happy result of a chance conversation at an event.

******

Rahul Bhasin, a client servicing manager at a well-known advertising agency, got chatting with the person on the adjacent seat on a flight from Mumbai to Bengaluru. The person turned out to be the CEO of a well-known IT company who offered to introduce Bhasin to his team. This serendipitous encounter landed Bhasin with a consulting assignment with the company a few months down the line.

Such experiences of positive outcomes emanating from serendipitous encounters with strangers are not uncommon. But is it just a stroke of good luck that leads to these positive outcomes?

What is luck anyway?

Dr Richard Wiseman,[1] Professor of public understanding of psychology at the University of Hertfordshire and author of *The Luck Factor: The Scientific Study of the Lucky Mind*, did an interesting study to understand the phenomenon of luck.

He invited two groups of people to volunteer for the study—one, comprising people who considered themselves exceptionally lucky and, second, including those who thought that they had been unusually unlucky, being struck by misfortune at regular junctures of life. The volunteers came from very diverse educational and professional backgrounds.

Wiseman administered a comprehensive, well-designed questionnaire to the two groups to understand whether there was something inherently different about their characteristics and traits. The subjects were asked to read a number of statements and score them on a 5-point scale based on how true they felt the statements to be. One of the statements on the questionnaire was: 'I sometimes chat to strangers when queuing in the supermarket or bank.'

And guess what? The respondents who seemed to experience a lot of 'luck' in their lives scored much higher on the statement compared to the respondents in the other category!

Dr Wiseman's research found that people were not born lucky or unlucky, and that luck was neither a magical ability nor the result of random chance. 'Lucky' people are simply more effective in the way they think and behave, which generates more positive results for them. They tend to notice chance opportunities, leverage their intuition for making 'right' decisions, expect positive outcomes and show far greater resilience in adverse situations. These characteristics work in concert to create positive outcomes for them.

Thus, openness to engaging with people, along with confidence, optimism and resilience could lead to chance encounters resulting in mutually beneficial relationships. However, you can't really depend on serendipity to create situations for you to meet people and build your network. Given the importance of relationships in achieving your goals and advancing your career, networking calls for a strategic approach.

Strategic Networking

Your network deserves a far more serious thought in terms of where it stands and where it needs to be in the light of your current and future goals. It would be pertinent to introspect and figure out whether your network encompasses people who will support you in the smooth turnout of your daily deliverables and those who will advocate and mentor you, support your ideas, help you navigate through the organization's political dynamics, contribute towards enhancing your knowledge and skills, point you to potential opportunities and provide you emotional support and energy. This entails taking stock of the current shape and size of your network, critiquing it, thinking strategically about how it needs to grow and designing an action plan to reorient it towards facilitating your career growth.

The Four-step Networking Plan

Follow the four-step networking framework discussed below for revitalizing, invigorating and reorienting your network.

1. *Map your current network*

   It is unlikely that you are starting this exercise from ground zero, since you already have a network of some form or design. The logical first step, therefore, is to capture or map your current network.

2. *Analyse your network*

   As a next step, evaluate your current network. Think about whether it will serve you well in the context of your goals. Does it encompass elements of operational, personal and accelerator networks discussed in Chapter 5? Do you see any gaps? Do you see redundancies? How will you fix these?

3. *Engage and add value*

   Once you have spotted the gaps and identified people, you could help bridge these, work out an action plan for engaging with them.

Figure 6.1. The Four-step Networking Plan

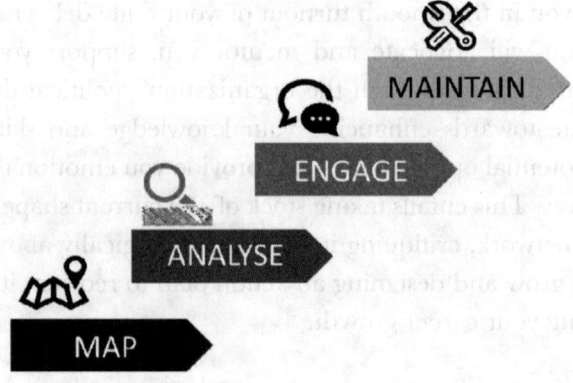

4. *Maintain your network*

Constantly under the pressure of time, we tend to engage more with people who are of immediate value in the context of our current deliverables and goals, often overlooking relationships developed in the past. Relationships, unless nourished and nurtured, are liable to fade, translating into a waste of time and effort invested in building them in the first place. This step is about ways to keeping those relationships active.

Step 1: Map Your Current Network

Use the template in Figure 6.2 to map your current network. Categorize people in terms of the three networks discussed earlier.

1. *Operational network*

People who provide support for your day-to-day tasks and deliverables.

Figure 6.2. Map Your Network

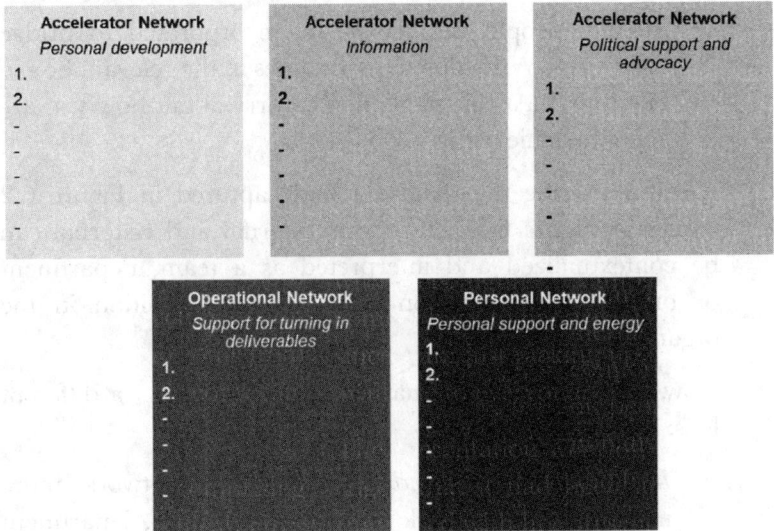

2. *Accelerator network*

People who provide information, political support and advocacy, mentorship and opportunities for development (knowledge, skills and developmental assignments).

3. *Personal network*

People who provide support and energy and opportunities to pursue common interests.

Step 2: Analyse Your Network

Identify Gaps

- Use the pointers below to analyse your current network.

    o Write down the top three business results or goals that you are hoping to achieve in the next two years.

    o Evaluate your network as mapped in Figure 6.2 in the context of these goals.

    o Do you see any gaps or shortfalls?

    o Identify people who could be incorporated to bridge these gaps. Write down their names in the relevant box in Figure 6.2. At this stage, don't worry about how you are going to achieve this.

- Next, transcribe the data you had captured in Figure 6.2 earlier to Figure 6.3. The terms Internal and External can be contextualized and interpreted as a team, department or organization based on your role and position in the organizational structure.

- Now, introspect and evaluate your network from a different lens:

    o *Internal or external inclination*—Is your network more inclined towards people in your own function, department or organization? Or have you developed relationships outside these entities? For instance, do you have connections in other departments, other locations and other organizations?

o *Hierarchy*—Does your network span across hierarchical levels? Do you have relationships that you can leverage at different levels in the organization or is it skewed towards a particular level?

• Do you see any gaps or shortfalls? Can you think of people you should reach out to who can render your network more balanced? Add their names in Figure 6.3.

• Having done this exercise with thousands of people, I have noticed the following themes.

o Often caught in the 'my task, my team and I' syndrome, people tend to remain task focused, underestimating

Figure 6.3. Analyse Your Network

INTERNAL		
Senior	Peer	Junior
EXTERNAL		
Senior	Peer	Junior

the value of a supportive ecosystem and seldom plan to develop their networks consciously and strategically.

o   Most people have a robust operational network since this is the network they were placed in by virtue of their job role in the organizational structure. These relationships, however, may not always be well nourished.

o   People generally have a robust personal network, comprising family and friends at work and outside, whose support they can depend on.

o   People tend to fall short with respect to their accelerator network—people who can be instrumental in their professional development.

o   People tend to have networks that are focused inwards, gravitating toward their peers and juniors, people in their functions and departments and people within their organization.

Imbalanced networks do not serve well in accomplishing goals or in successful critical career transitions. As you move towards leadership roles, your network must reorient itself externally and towards the future. What you need is a diverse network that is cross functional, cross hierarchical, cross organizational and cross geographical. Rob Cross and Robert J. Thomas,[2] authors of 'Managing Yourself: A Smarter Way to Network', a *Harvard Business Review* article, rightly say, 'The executives who consistently rank in the top 20% of their companies in both performance and well-being have diverse but select networks made up of high-quality relationships with people who come from several different spheres and from up and down the corporate hierarchy.'

So, aim to develop a well-rounded core network comprising 12 to 18 people that is cross functional, cross hierarchical, cross

Figure 6.4. Network Structure

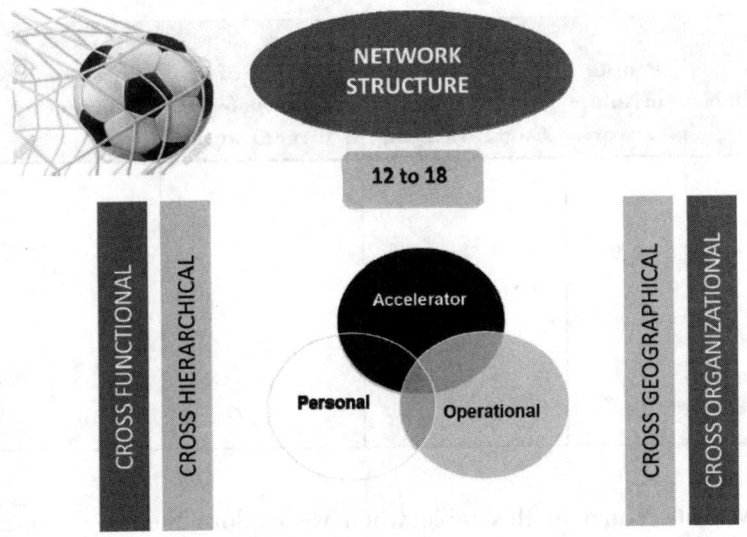

organizational and cross geographical, which will support your career advancement as well as your emotional and physical well-being.

Asses the Maturity of Your Relationships

1. Use Table 6.1 to list down people—those currently on your network and those whom you would like to add, as captured in Figure 6.3.

2. Rate the strength of your current relationship with each person on a 5-point scale where:

   a. 1—Never interacted

   b. 5—Strong relationship

3. To what extent would you like to cultivate the relationship? Rate the target strength of the relationship.

Table 6.1: Relationship Maturity Assessment

S. N.	People in Your Network	Maturity of the Relationship—Current Rating	Maturity of the Relationship—Target Rating	Strategy for Connecting

We will return to this table when we explore Step 3 of your networking plan.

Identify Redundancies

The idea of identifying redundancies or 'delayering' your network is likely to evoke a sense of discomfort. One is uneasy with the idea of 'unfriending' a person. But given that relationships take time and energy to cultivate, both of which are limited resources, it is judicious to prioritize and be selective about how and where you invest these resources. Moreover, 'delayering' does not mean severing ties. It just means spending less time engaging with someone, as there is another relationship more important in the current context that needs a greater investment of time. Consider the following examples.

During one of my corporate stints, I used to engage frequently with four colleagues in the department on account of mutual dependencies for meeting our individual and departmental goals. We engaged socially as well, meeting for lunch on most days and stepping out to the nearby mall on Fridays. In the course of time, one of our group buddies grew spectacularly in the organization with his career graph taking a sharp upward turn. Soon he was promoted to a very senior role in recognition of his contribution, potential and the value that he brought to the table.

Soon after his promotion, he moved into a cabin on a different floor. Thereafter, he was seldom available for small talk and subsequently stopped coming for lunch to the cafeteria, preferring to eat by himself in his cabin. He had in fact 'delayered' us. It did not feel good at the time because it seemed like the 'forgetting old pals' syndrome playing out. But in retrospect, I understand that with his expanded role and new responsibilities, he was playing on a much wider field with a host of new stakeholders. He had to forge new relationships and build a new and expanded ecosystem. And with limited time and energy, he was right in prioritizing and fine-tuning his network.

****

Neerja, an executive in an e-commerce company, once spoke to me about a friend and her former colleague, who often called her to engage in career-related conversations, revolving around job responsibilities, increments and promotion. She would often ask questions about Neerja's annual increments with responses like, 'Oh! only that much? Why didn't you ask for more? You know X is getting this and Y that. Why don't you consider applying elsewhere?' She never failed to mention how much better off, compared to Neerja, she was on all these parameters. Neerja would feel drained, stressed out and demotivated every time she spoke to this friend, unable to focus on work for the next few hours. 'Perhaps it is time for you to 'delayer' this friend,' I had suggested. The idea was not to cut her off completely, but to reduce the frequency and the amount of time spent with her. After all, you need people around you who will energize and motivate you, rather than sap your energy by generating anxiety.

This is corroborated by a study[3] done by Dr Nicholas Christakis of Harvard Medical School and Dr James Fowler of the University of California in San Diego, which shows that those associated with happy people tend to be more cheerful and have a better sense of well-being. Strangely, a person's happiness can also influence the happiness of people who are up to three degrees of separation from them, that is, your happiness can rub off positively on a friend's friend's friend! And the closer you are to a person emotionally and physically, the stronger the influence.

Step 3: Engage and Add Value

Once you have evaluated your network in terms of the gaps, identified people who can seal these gaps and evaluated the strength of your existing relationships, the next logical step is to reach out to people and engage with them for building and strengthening your relationships, thus, developing a more balanced network that will serve you well in realizing your endeavours.

Robert Cialdini,[4] author of the international bestseller *Influence: The Psychology of Persuasion*, says that we tend to be supportive of those whom we like. And we like those who are helpful, who appreciate us and pay us compliments, and who are similar to us. Besides, we are drawn to people who exude energy and don a positive demeanour. So, leverage these simple principles of persuasion science to connect with people. Consider the examples given below.

Compliment People: Strike an Instant Chord

I walked into our new office bracing myself for the usual teething problems—connectivity issues, malfunctioning infrastructure and discrepancies in space allocation. But I was pleasantly surprised to see everything working to perfection without the slightest glitch. Putting on my laptop, I dashed off an email to the IT and the administration teams complimenting them for their wonderful job, marking a copy to the CEO. The impact of this acknowledgement and appreciation was palpable in their smiling faces that shone with pride. This small gesture helped me strike an instant chord with the teams, and I noticed a distinct uptick in their responsiveness to my team's requirements subsequently.

The art of complimenting is a simple, powerful and a highly underutilized social skill that generates a sense of instant positivity, warmth and well-being, not just for the person receiving the compliment but also for the one paying it. An authentic compliment can trigger an instant connect, stimulate conversation and set the stage for taking the connection forward. But it takes an observant eye to discern a praiseworthy situation, and willingness and confidence for articulating and delivering a compliment.

Focus on Giving

Bob Burg and John Mann,[5] authors of *Go-Givers Sell More*, have articulated the basis of networking as 'shifting your focus from *getting* to *giving*'. When trying to connect with someone, it would be pertinent to ask, 'How can I support this person? What can I do that would be useful for them?' Nailing this down and offering the person something that they value forms a solid foundation for a relationship. See the examples below.

I follow the practice of reaching out to industry colleagues— business heads, HR heads and CEOs—to gather their views and experiences and incorporate these in my articles that I contribute to different publications from time to time. Most people readily give me an audience, because embedded in this request is an implicit acknowledgment of their knowledge, expertise and experience. Besides, being quoted in a publication gives them, as well as the organization they represent, a fair amount of visibility. What does it give me? Besides lending credibility to my stories, these conversations keep me abreast of current industry practices, policies and events in general. This enhances my knowledge, adds new dimensions to my perspective and enables me to engage in conversations with people in a more informed manner.

******

I once did a pro bono coaching engagement for a senior finance manager in a bank. He had been struggling with a few personal and professional issues that were posing roadblocks in his success. As I got him to introspect during the course of those 10 sessions, he obtained some valuable insights and answers and experienced positive outcomes when he translated these to concrete actions. He became one of my greatest advocates thereafter. By providing me a valuable opportunity to hone my coaching skills, it turned out to be a mutually beneficial engagement, strengthening our relationship in the process.

****

Manasi, a senior consultant in an advertising agency, takes it upon herself to coach young marketing managers when they are tasked with writing award entries for various advertising awards events. She invests quality time coaching, cajoling, reprimanding, shouting, yelling and browbeating them to come up with recommendations that are really stellar. Since this grind usually gets people to a podium finish, with its concomitant thrill and excitement, they look up to Manasi, embracing her with all her idiosyncrasies. And others, too, want to be on Manasi's network when they hear about her informal coaching engagements with their colleagues.

But what was in it for Manasi? First, it helped her develop a reputation for mentoring and shaping people, thus establishing her leadership skills. Second, it provided her an opportunity to understand the younger generation, getting insights into their aspirations, goals, priorities and communication style and what really made them tick.

Occasionally, she also receives some valuable technology tips from them—a manifestation of 'reverse mentoring'.

Mutual benefit, therefore, constitutes a strong basis for any relationship, just like the symbiotic relationship between the clownfish and the sea anemone.

Meet Informally: A Lot Can Happen over Coffee

People tend to be more relaxed in an informal, non-work-related environment, which really lends itself to easy conversations, small talk and casual engagement. This is the perfect set-up for getting to know and forging connections with people.

Dhanda, a senior client servicing manager at a global advertising agency, shared an anecdote where his manager had recommended that he meet up clients informally. It was more of a mandate actually, as it was documented as one of the action items on his goal sheet for the year.

Sceptical about the idea, he was tormented with thoughts about the client's likely reaction to his invite. 'He is bound to think that I am sucking up!' he thought. With great trepidation, he invited one of his clients and his wife out for dinner. Much to his amazement, far from being an ordeal, it turned out to be an enjoyable evening for Dhanda and his wife. They had a ball of a time conversing with the other couple about cricket, trekking, music, the country's economic landscape—stuff outside of work. Having identified commonalities, they were able to connect at a personal level and continued meeting informally thereafter. This proved to be a turning point in their relationship and went a long way in ironing out several work-related issues that were creating an annoying noise in an otherwise smooth working relationship.

Similarly, when Dhanda started the practice of meeting the creative team members informally, he started appreciating their perspective, pain areas and drivers and used the opportunity to communicate the client's context and his own viewpoints to them. This mutual understanding helped them think like a team, work in unison and craft out solutions that were in the clients' best interest.

*****

After I had completed my meetings with the business and HR head at a bank, recently, I decided to spend some time with the HR executives, who fortunately were willing to meet me at a short notice. I was very fascinated to learn that one of them was a trained and practising hypnotist. She happily spoke about the concept of hypnosis, how she had stumbled into the field, the process of hypnotism and the benefits from the practice. The conversation then veered towards COVID-19, how it had started, the latest count and the bank's business continuity plan to deal with it. I learnt that the bank had a second location in Mumbai which they were planning to equip and galvanize to action. This informal conversation went a long way in breaking the ice, and subsequently, I noticed that their responsiveness to my messages had gone up several notches higher.

We expect people to play their roles in accordance with the standard operating procedure, as in a factory context. But that's not how it plays out in real life, since the actions of people are guided by their fears, cheers and tears, their triggers and motivators and their goals and aspirations. Identifying and dealing with these are important in order to engage with them, manage them, influence them and garner their support. And this happens best when meeting people in informal set-ups.

Diversify Your Group

Openness to engaging with a wider group of diverse people paves the way for developing a wider network.

'Two years ago you would invariably found me at my desk, plodding away at work, except during the lunch and tea breaks when I would hang around with my group of five colleagues,' says Shyamla Chetri, a manager in the technology team of a global IT company. 'I was sensing that in many ways I was limiting myself by restricting to a single group,' she added.

'Shortly thereafter, on account of a change in my role, I was fortunate to get an opportunity to work with a different team, at a different desk, on a different floor and a vastly different environment. This is one of the best things that happened to me, as it got me to look at things afresh, and propelled me to step out of my comfort zone,' she continued. Once the initial introductions were done, she made a conscious attempt to invest time engaging with people rather than being glued to her desk all day. She started taking interest in getting to know them better—their interests and areas of expertise. Similarly, she was now also more inclined to talk about her skills, knowledge and leisure pursuits. More importantly, she refrained from restricting herself to any particular group as she had done in the past. She made it a practice to walk into the cafeteria and join different groups for lunch. 'This small change, helped me interact with so many different people, learnt new things, build my network and get access to the buzz around the organizational environment,' she said.

Reach out to People

Sometimes, all it takes to connect with people is to reach out to them. But we are often held back by a constellation of reasons like inertia, lack of time, disinclination towards stepping out of the comfort zone and fear of rejection. Given below are experiences of people who did make time, gathered courage and took the initiative to reach out to people; thereby enriching their network and benefiting from new opportunities.

Struck by the entrepreneurial bug and unexcited at the prospect of a 9–5 job, Mitesh Kumar was already toying with the idea of a start-up during his second year of management at the Indian Institute of Management at Ahmedabad. One of the subjects that Mitesh had immensely enjoyed at the Institute was strategy. The subject was taught by one of the leading IT honchos, Prakash Yadav, who had the knack of weaving in interesting anecdotes from his enormously rich industry experience around the otherwise dull theoretical concepts to render the classes amazingly interesting.

Keen to bounce off the start-up idea with Prakash, Mitesh was trying to get some personal time with him. He tried catching his attention by being vocal in class, asking questions, participating actively in class discussions and hanging around to engage in after-class discussions, but that one-on-one time with Prakash continued to evade him. Prakash had started the practice of breakfast meetings to engage with students one-on-one. But unfortunately, Mitesh was unable to get a slot on this forum. Desperate for a conversation, Mitesh had a brainwave on the last day of the program when Prakash was slated to leave Ahmedabad. He mustered courage and requested Prakash if he may drive with him and engage in a conversation on the way to the airport. Lady luck smiled as Prakash readily agreed.

The meeting turned out to be very fruitful, as Prakash gave him some invaluable insights and unravelled some additional dimensions which helped Mitesh sharpen his idea further. In fact, Prakash was so impressed with the potential of his idea that he offered to fund his venture once he was ready with the prototype.

Mitesh continued to maintain his contact with Prakash, dropping him an occasional mail briefing him on his start-up, asking questions and engaging him in discussions on topics of mutual interest.

*****

Santoshi, a young professional and a foreign university MBA aspirant, has recently secured admission in an Ivy League school. She attributes her success with the elaborate application process to the useful insights and support she had garnered from those who had undergone the process themselves. She started by identifying a 100 people on LinkedIn—current students and alumni of her target colleges. She reached out to them with a message, 'Hi, I am hoping for a phone conversation with you, at your convenience, to understand how you went about your MBA application process.' Very hesitant initially, she braced herself for rejection, firmly telling herself that in the worst-case scenario people will not respond. But to her pleasant surprise, she found that people were very forthcoming and willing to talk and share their experiences. She managed to speak with 50 of the 100 people she had initially approached.

These conversations helped her narrow down on target colleges and obtain beneficial tips on what had worked for them and, in hindsight, what they wished they had done different. For instance, she learnt that while 92 per cent students on campus had been placed the previous year, there were certainly some limitations for those holding an Indian passport. Further, she understood the benefit of leveraging a consultant for facilitating the process and benefited from working with one. In addition, she got some insights on preference of schools for specific skill sets. For example, she learnt that one particular school looked for evidence of collaboration on the application, while another looked for quantitative skills and a third counted diversity as an important element in its selection criteria. 'It would have been impossible to obtain such insights from other regular sources,' she said. Some of people she had reached out to had even offered to review the essays she had drafted for the applications and she ended up forging long-term connections with many of them.

*****

At her annual performance review, Surekha, a senior manager at an IT company, was told by her manager that while she was recognized as an outstanding delivery lead within her own group, she had little or no visibility within the global delivery organization, which comprised 10 delivery verticals in different locations across the globe. Her manager identified one particular delivery head, Anil Dhanda, who worked out of the same location and tasked her with engaging with him.

Surekha was extremely uncomfortable at the prospect of soliciting a meeting with a senior colleague. 'I had no agenda,' she exclaimed! The task weighed heavily on her as a couple of months frittered by. At the following quarterly operations conference, she found herself in the same meeting room as Dhanda. Mustering all her courage, she accosted him saying, 'May I request you for a meeting as I have been tasked with connecting with you.' Looking at her quizzically, he foxed her with a counter question. 'Which companies are known for innovation?' he asked. 'Google and Apple,' was her prompt response. 'Why Google and Apple? What held you back from naming our company?' he asked, to which she lamely replied, 'Well, that's my perception.' 'Can you substantiate it? Can you meet me with a presentation on why Google and Apple are perceived as innovative and suggestions for our company to step into that league?' 'Of course,' she replied, not sure what she had let herself into.

She researched the two companies, reading several articles over the next few days and prepared a solid presentation fortified with facts, figures, examples and stories. The thought that kept coming back to her was, 'What value would this presentation add, since I am just picking up information from the internet which is available to everyone?'

The presentation went off extremely well and Dhanda acknowledged that it had been an eye-opener for him in many ways. Impressed with her presentation, Dhanda invited Surekha to be a part of his innovation core team. This not only gave her visibility within the global delivery organization but also opened up other opportunities. She was asked to lead 'On Campus', an initiative to engage with colleges to facilitate the recruitment of freshers. Impressed with her performance, Dhanda also proposed her name for leading 'Elevate'—a forum for recruiting, retaining and developing women, in addition to providing networking opportunities. There was fierce competition from other contenders, but Dhanda firmly stood by her.

Surekha attributes her success to Dhanda's political support and advocacy. 'But the first step really was to overcome my own hesitation in reaching out to a senior stakeholder and subsequently reinforcing my credibility through good performance,' remarked Surekha.

Respond to Requests

At times, all it takes to strike a connection is to overcome your hesitation and respond to a request. Sounds simple and highly doable, but many an opportunity is lost because of hesitation, indecision and vacillation between 'should I' or 'shouldn't I' as shown in the example below.

Bhavesh Mahajan, the COO of an insurance company, had once written to a well-known author, complimenting him on a new book that he had released, with a message, 'Wonderful book. I look forward to meeting you some day.'

The author had written back saying, 'It would be a pleasure to meet you for lunch whenever you are in Chennai next.' Debating whether to take him up on his invite, Mahajan was troubled by thoughts like 'Did he invite me because of my position in the company? Is he sucking up to me? Will it seem like I am sucking up to him if I accept the invite?' Dithering thus, Mahajan did not respond to the author's invite and lost an opportunity to forge an important connection. 'Anyone else in my place would have made a special trip to Chennai to have lunch with the author,' remarked Mahajan.

Be Persistent

Sometimes, it takes persistence to connect with people as shown in the instances below.

A participant at one of my training sessions had shared an interesting anecdote about his friend, John, who was seeking the dealership for cement when a business house had just introduced white cement in Mumbai. He had put in his application and was trying to meet the company's CEO. He tried hard to set up a meeting for over a month but to no avail. In the meantime, he learnt that the CEO was accustomed to taking walks at 6 AM daily at Worli Sea Face. John jumped into action and tuned his own walk timing to synchronize with that of the CEO. Befriending the CEO during these walks over time, he shared his credentials and succeeded in setting up the meeting that had long eluded him.

****

A petrol station proprietor had been struggling to set up a meeting with a director at Oil and Natural Gas Commission for quite a while. On one of his rounds at the director's office, he was told by his assistant for the 100th time that the director could not meet him. And this time, the reason she cited was that he was travelling to Kolkata the following morning. The petrol station proprietor got the clue that he was looking for. He leveraged his sources to obtain the flight details and booked himself on the same flight, even obtaining a seat adjacent to that of the director, thus getting to meet him mid-air. This was indeed a resourceful and novel approach to making a connection!

Be Visible, Be Credible

Visibility facilitates networking. People would tend to be more receptive to your call to connect if they already know you as a result of your writing, speaking, training and other forms of engagement at various organizational and industry forums, your participation in cross-functional projects and your engagement on the social media. This will be explored in detail in the next section on 'Visibility'.

CALL FOR ACTION

- **How readily do you compliment people?**

  o Make a conscious effort to compliment or thank <u>two</u> people every day for the next one week and document your experience.

  o How easy or difficult was it for you to:

    - Discern an appropriate context for paying a compliment

    - Articulate the compliment

    - Deliver the compliment. Did it come easily and naturally, or did you have to brace yourself for it?

  o What was the reaction of the person who was complimented?

  o How did you feel after paying the compliment?

- **Strategy for connecting**

  o You had listed people in your current network and identified those whom you would like to add to your network in Table 6.1.

o   Based on the discussion in this chapter review the list in Table 6.1 again and identify an appropriate strategy for:

- Connecting with a person whom you want to add to your network and

- Strengthening your relationships with a person already on your network.

Step 4: Maintain Your Network

Earlier in the chapter, we spoke about how critical it is to evaluate and reshape your core network for accomplishing your goals. In fact, it is important to perform this exercise periodically to keep your network relevant and useful for meeting your dynamic needs.

In reality, your network spans far beyond this core group, encompassing the web of relationships that you have developed along the way. But relationships tend to fade and wear out, unless nourished regularly. Since network maintenance, which is about nurturing these relationships, requires an investment of time and effort, it often falls prey to the more pressing day-to-day transactions and engagement with people who are of immediate value. We tend to lose sight of these past relationships that had been painstakingly cultivated at some point. Think of people whom you had worked with in your former organizations. When was the last time you connected with them? How about people in the department that you had worked in earlier? Or the people with whom you had exchanged business cards and pleasantries in the last networking event you had attended? By neglecting these past relationships, you may be depriving yourself of a host of potential opportunities. For instance, how comfortable would you feel reaching out to a former colleague, now the head of marketing in an organization, if you haven't connected with him/her for the last nine years? How receptive would a former colleague be to your call for information if you have been out of touch for several years?

Maintaining your network is important and it entails an investment of time. So how do you achieve this, given that you are already stretched for time and energy? This need not be a difficult exercise, if done intentionally with some planning and discipline.

As a first step, capture your entire network on a worksheet and prioritize people based on their relevance and importance from the perspective of your deliverables and current and future goals and allocate time based on priority. Next, adopt one or more of the following easy ways that are light on time and energy to keep your connections going.

Show That You Care

Communicate with people in various contexts.

- Send a 'I hope you are safe' message to people in a city struck by a natural calamity.

- Occasionally, send a 'Haven't communicated in a long time. Hope all's well' message to remain connected with people.

- Establish a quick connect with people in a different city when travelling to that city, saying something like, 'Hi, just landed in your city. Thought I'd say a quick hi. Hope all's well.'

Share Relevant Content

Share any articles, podcasts or videos that you think would be of interest to them. For instance, I share all my published articles with my entire network. I am not sure whether people actually read them, but it certainly keeps them abreast of the broad topics I am writing on and helps build recall value.

Recommend a Book or an Event

Share the details of a book, conference, seminar or any other forum that you chance upon which you think may be of interest to them.

Write a Congratulatory Message

Appreciation makes people tick. It drives spirits up and helps strike a positive chord. Congratulate people when they are promoted or have made a successful career move. LinkedIn is an easy source to get this information. Track the media and write a congratulatory message when you see the person or their company in news for achieving a milestone, declaring stellar financial results, announcing expansion plans, launching a new product or engaging in a corporate social responsibility (CSR) activity.

Engage over Coffee

Meeting people for coffee is an effective way to keep the connection going. Say something like, 'Hi, I am coming your side of town next week. Thought we could catch up over coffee. I can drop in at your office if that works.' Exchange pleasantries, indulge in small talk and share industry news.

Be Helpful

I have often received requests like:

- My friend wants to make a career in marketing. She wants to talk to someone in the field for an insider's view. Can you help out?

- My niece is looking for an internship. Can you connect her with some companies?

- My son wants to pursue a program in public policy. Can you guide him on the job prospects?

You may not have the wherewithal to address these requests, but surely you can find someone who does. Invest some time scouting around for people in your direct or indirect network who can help and connect them. This small gesture will go a long way in strengthening your relationship.

Leverage the Social Media

Stay connected on LinkedIn or Twitter. Comment on people's posts and join the discussion by adding another dimension to what they have posted. Re-post or retweet their post to share it with a wider audience.

Invite People to Your Company Forums

Another effective way to keep in touch is to invite a person as a keynote speaker, a panellist or simply as a participant to a conference, annual day event or a marketing event organized by your company.

Greet People on Festivals

Sending new year and festivals greetings is another way of keeping in touch with people. Use technology to personalize your message for better impact. People are more likely to pay attention and warm up to a message addressed to them by name than one broadcast to a large group.

Be cognizant of the following points for greater effectiveness.

- *Be audience-centric*

   Put some thought into and use your judgment to decide which tool of engagement would be appropriate for different people of your network.

- *Don't overdo*

   Don't put off people by connecting once too often as that may turn counterproductive, doing more harm than good.

- *Be authentic*

   Be genuinely interested in people. Authenticity is important in every engagement, whether you are appreciating, thanking, congratulating or helping.

- *Be consistent*

   It is important to be consistent and regular in engaging with people. Set up a plan in terms of the frequency and tool of engagement.

- *Be cautious*

   When sending an email message to a large group, remember to put everyone in 'bcc'. I had once sent an article to 400 people, inadvertently putting everyone in 'cc'. One of the recipients had responded to the article with a 'reply all' thus sharing his response with 400 others marked on the mail. People had not taken kindly to it.

- *Don't be disappointed*

   Don't be ruffled if people don't respond to your efforts at maintaining the connection. Remember that people are busy. But continue your efforts relentlessly and you are bound to experience a positive shift in the power of your network over time.

Remember that relationship building needs to be an ongoing process and relationships need to be built much in advance of when you need them. Just-in-time relationships don't work. So, focus on building the connection and consider any concomitant benefits as a happy corollary.

CALL FOR ACTION

- Draw up a database of all the people in your network whom you would like to remain connected with.

- Segment the list in order of priority— high, medium, low.

- Identify the engagement tools you would like to use for each segment.

- Define the frequency with which you will connect.

- Serendipitous networking comprises chance encounters with people that lead to mutually beneficial outcomes.

- A strategic approach to networking is needed to build a network that will serve you well for expanding your professional options and enhancing your general well-being.

- Use a 4-step networking plan to develop a network in the context of your immediate and future goals.

1. *Map your current network*

   Start by mapping your current network.

2. *Analyse your network*

   Use the following questions to analyse your current network against the backdrop of your goals.

   - Does it incorporate elements of an operational, personal and an accelerator network?

   - Does it incorporate people across levels, functions and locations?

   - Are there any gaps that you need to bridge?

   - Are there any redundancies?

- Identify people whom you should add or strengthen your relationship with, to render your network more robust and balanced.

3. *Engage and add value*

- Work out a plan to establish connections and strengthen your relationship with people.

- Leverage a combination of strategies to engage with people.

   o Compliment people

   o Be helpful

   o Meet people informally

   o Diversify the group that you hang out with

   o Reach out to people

   o Respond positively to requests for connection

   o Be persistent

4. *Maintain your network*

- Maintaining your network is an important step towards keeping relationships alive and thriving.

- Segment your network in order of priority.

- Use one or more of the following ways to keep your connections going.

   o Keep in touch with relevant messages

   o Share relevant content

   o Recommend an appropriate book, event or forum

   o Congratulate and compliment

   o Meet people informally

o Respond positively to calls for help

o Leverage the social media

o Greet people on festivals

References

1. Wiseman R. The luck factor: the scientific study of the lucky mind. Denver: Talking Books; 2003.
2. Cross R, Thomas RJ. Managing yourself: a smarter way to network. Harv Bus Rev [Internet]. July–Aug 2011 Available from: https://hbr.org/2011/07/managing-yourself-a-smarter-way-to-network
3. Eaton C. Surround yourself with happy people to be happy. University of New Hampshire [Internet]. 15 October 2012. Available from: https://www.unh.edu/healthyunh/blog/2012/10/surround-yourself-happy-people-be-happy
4. Cialdini R. Influence: the psychology of persuasion. Melbourne: Harper Business; 1984.
5. Burg B, Mann JD. Go givers sell more. New York: Penguin Publishing Group; 2010.

Chapter 7

Networking a Room

Networking for Introverts

You have just received an email invite for the prestigious 'Women in IT' conference to mark the International Women's Day (or any other relevant conference related to your domain). How do you react to the invite?

1. Your face lights up and you are excited at the thought of meeting people and exchanging ideas.

2. You are not excited, but you think it is a great opportunity to meet people.

3. You flinch at the idea of jumping into a sea of humanity, smiling and making small talk with strangers.

If your answer is 3, then you are not alone! You are a part of approximately 50 per cent of the world's population that is made up of 'introverts', a term popularized by Karl Jung to describe people who are focused more on their inner thoughts and feelings rather than social interactions. According to Susan Cain, author of *Quiet: The Power of Introverts in a World That Can't Stop Talking*,[1] introverts work best in a quiet, minimally stimulating environment, preferring to engage in solo activities like reading, studying, designing and meditating. Extroverts, in contrast, thrive when exposed to higher degrees of stimulation through social interaction in meetings, conversations and team activities.

Why is that so? The answer lies in biology!

Dr Marti Olsen Laney, author of *The Introvert Advantage: How to Thrive in an Extrovert World*,[2] explains that the brain of an introvert is inherently wired towards a higher degree of environmental sensitivity. In addition, transmission of information takes longer, as the neural pathways, along which it flows, are longer in an introvert's brain. As a result, the brain of an introvert has to work harder and needs a higher dash of dopamine to process external stimuli like loud noise and crowded events, causing uneasiness and taking a toll on energy.

Extroverts, on the other hand, are endowed with a nervous system designed to expend energy, as a result of which they are constantly seeking dopamine-enhancing stimuli like conversations, meetings and new experiences.

I met Shruti Bhaskar, an assistant vice president, operations, at a multinational bank at one of my training sessions. She shared a personal anecdote about the time when she had been nominated to attend an IT conference. She was flattered as she was one of the privileged few to have been nominated for the event. She was also aware of the big opportunity that this presented in terms of learning about the current IT trends, hearing different perspectives, thoughts and viewpoints, meeting people and building connections. Nonetheless, she found the prospect distasteful and even toyed with the idea of opting out.

But, encouraged by her manager, she mustered the energy and the motivation to go to the conference. All was well as long as she was sitting in the audience hearing the talks and panel discussions. It was the breaks between the sessions, potentially the 'networking' slots meant for meeting and greeting, making introductions, engaging in small talk and exchanging business cards that she found nerve-racking. She decided to follow the practice of walking out during these breaks and ensconced in a shady corner, engaging in telephonic conversations with her mother and friends, away from the din of the networking scene.

What can introverts like Shruti do to leverage these opportunities?

Be Who You Are

If large conferences, big crowds and parties deplete your energy and you are likely to return from these events exhausted and feeling drained, then it is really not worth your while to go there in the first place. Going against the grain of your personality is not likely to work.

A senior advertising professional, counted among the top 25 most influential people in Indian advertising by *Economic Times Brand Equity*, one of India's foremost sources of information and news on the marketing and advertising industries, remarked, 'Parties and networking events just don't work for me and I generally keep away from such events, except in extraordinary circumstances when excusing myself is just not an option. People in my ecosystem have accepted my distaste for parties and have come to respect it.'

When asked whether this has hurt his career in any way, since the advertising industry is known for heavy socializing, his response was, 'Not really, because I say 'no' to parties and networking events, not to relationship building. I acknowledge and advocate the importance of forging relationships, which facilitate your work by acting as social lubricants,' he said. He went on to explain his modus operandi for connecting with people. 'I prefer meeting people in small groups or one-on-one over lunch or coffee. This allows you some quality time to engage in a meaningful conversation and really connect in the true sense.'

I met a well-known corporate lawyer, who has played top roles in multinational organizations in the legal space. She said to me, 'I am not a networker in that sense. Casual conversations or banter with people whom I don't know, all in the name of net-working, are not only unexciting, they are off-putting. I see no sense in it as it doesn't energize me. I prefer to connect with a few select people over a quiet dinner at home, or over a coffee or lunch in small groups to develop some meaningful, long term relationships.'

Step Out of Your Comfort Zone

One of my training program participants once shared that he tended to be very energized, enthusiastic and perfectly at ease when engaging in work-related conversations. But was very uncomfort-able making small talk and would almost never engage in those getting-to-know-each-other, rapport building exchanges.

'For a very long time I used to avoid going to conferences and other socio-business events. But with time and maturity, I saw merit in attending these events and engaging in non-work conversations for building connections. Having bought into the idea, I took the initiative to learn the requisite skills and overcame my awkwardness with some practice. Even today I have to brace myself for such occasions. But I make a conscious effort to step out of my comfort zone and frankly I have realized that it's not too tough. And I have experienced the benefits which are a big motivator,' he said.

Explore Alternative Communication Channels

Others, who categorize themselves as introverts and are uncomfortable with face-to-face interaction, have successfully explored alternative channels like Twitter chats, LinkedIn or even phone calls which enable them to connect with people from the comfort of their drawing room.

Your Networking Toolkit

People, both introverts and extroverts, are often daunted by large conferences, big crowds and even internal organizational networking events because of their discomfort with approaching groups, engaging in small talk and having to make an 'impactful' introduction. This, however, is really about honing your communication skills and preparing for the event which can be easily achieved with some thought and practice.

Get Your Teeth into the Event

As a first step, get some information on the event in terms of the organizers, speakers and the theme of the event. Think about who you are likely to meet there—a current or a former colleague perhaps, or someone from the industry whom you know. It is worth spending time exploring this as it would give you the comfort of knowing someone at the event whom you could hang out with, rendering the prospect a little less daunting.

Goal Setting: Knowing the What, Why and How

Why are you going to the event? What is your goal? Is it to enhance your knowledge and learn more about the subject, communicate your credentials and gain visibility, connect with industry peers or forge new contacts? It could well be all of these.

Practice Your Introduction

I remember having made a hash of my introduction at a couple of events, earlier in my career. I recall having floundered for the right words, doing injustice to who I was and what I did and, in the process, losing a valuable opportunity to make a good impression. And first impressions do matter! The next time around, however, I spent some time preparing my introduction. I wrote down some points and, more importantly, rehearsed the piece so it rolled off my tongue smoothly and easily.

Figure out how you are going to introduce yourself in three or four sentences, an elevator pitch of sorts, touching upon your organization, role and areas of expertise and interests. But remember that the same introduction will not work in every context as it needs to be customized to the audience and the situation to be relevant and impactful.

Prepare for Small Talk

'Making small talk can have a big impact on your career,' John Baldoni,[3] author of 13 books on leadership, astutely observed in his 2010 article, 'Tips for Making Small Talk with Bigwigs' published in the *Harvard Business Review*.

Thomas W. Harrell,[4] Professor Emeritus, Graduate School of Business at Stanford University had conducted an interesting study tracking the careers of MBA students over a 20-year period after graduation. His objective was to identify personality traits that contributed to professional success (read compensation). His study found that success was more highly and consistently correlated with sociability than with grade point averages. This suggests that successful people tend to share a common trait in terms of their ability to make conversation with anyone—from CEOs, bosses, customers, receptionists down to the security guards and even strangers. People also tend to perceive good conversationalists as intelligent and confident.

Small talk is a quick, effective tool for connecting, rapport building and filling 'between-event' time spaces in a host of different contexts—training programs, conferences, seminars and official and social parties, or even chance meetings with people in the corridor, elevator or over lunch. The art of making small talk comes naturally to some, but it is really a skill that can be learnt and cultivated. Look through the points below.

- *Develop a mindset to engage.*

  It is important, first, to be interested in people and having a mindset to engage, and second, don a pleasant and open demeanour that encourages people to come forward and engage with you. So be interested and be interesting!

- *Be prepared with talking points.*

  Think through some talking points based on the event you are slated to attend. Don't worry too much about what you are going to say, think of some appropriate questions first.

  o Get a peek into the backgrounds and interests of people you are likely to meet at the event. Carry out a quick Google search to see if they, or the organizations they work for, have figured in the media recently. View their LinkedIn profiles. Then ask some appropriate questions like:

    — 'Hey, I read your article in *Economic Times* the other day!' followed by a few questions and comments about the article.

    — If a person has recently changed jobs—'How is the new job going? Are you settled? How is this different from what you were doing earlier?'

    — A person whose child is preparing for a degree at a foreign university—'When is Rupam leaving? Is she all set? What program has she enrolled for?'

- o Initiate a conversation with some generic remarks and questions related to the event, especially with people whom you don't know.

    - 'Have you attended this conference before?'

    - 'What did you think of the previous speaker?' Follow it up with a few points around the talk.

    - 'I hadn't expected such a large gathering!'

    - 'Where are you working?'

- o Ask questions related to their domain or industry. I have found this particularly useful for breaking the ice and getting to know my participants before commencing a training program. For instance:

    - 'I read about this new norm that has recently kicked in, mandating all listed companies to change their auditor every 10 years. How is this likely to impact your business?'

    - 'What is the range of products that you manufacture? Do you cater primarily to the domestic or foreign market? How's the business doing?'

    - 'I understand that there's been a change of leadership in your organization. What does that mean for you?'

    - 'I read that your bank is on an expansion spree. Which areas are you expanding in? Over what period are you likely to hire? What are the numbers?'

- o In addition, expand your knowledge of common current topics like the economy, the stock market, COVID-19 and its impact, sports, entertainment and the like to be able to participate and contribute to group conversations.

- *Listen intently—good listening works magic.*

  o Others may just be as weary of starting a conversation as you are. So, take the initiative and trigger a conversation by asking a question. Then sit back, relax and watch the other person do the heavy lifting of taking the conversation forward. People will talk quite willingly if they have a captive listener. Moreover, instead of struggling with what to say, they now have something concrete to talk about in response to your question.

  o Display your interest and involvement in the conversation by making eye contact, smiling, nodding, asking relevant questions and responding with remarks like 'how interesting', 'what a surprise', 'tell me more'. Listen to the total person. Observe. Watch out for both words and body language to get cues about whether the person is interested in continuing the engagement or would rather move on. Be tuned for topics of mutual interest as these could trigger further conversation. For instance,

    – If you see a person piling a mountain of rice and Thai curry on her plate, you could ask, 'Is Thai your favourite cuisine? It is mine too…. I would recommend this particular Thai restaurant located in one of the remote alleys in town, known for serving the most authentic and reasonably priced Thai food. I often go there with my family.'

    – 'From your accent, you don't sound like a Mumbaikar. Which part of the country are you from?'

    Remember that 75 per cent of small talk is about listening with interest.

- *Approach people—break the ice.*

  o To land at an event and not know anyone there can be intimidating. You have walked in suitably dressed, armed with your talking points, but how do you approach people? Who do you approach?

o   Your best bet initially is to approach a person who has turned in solo like you. So, scan the room and look out for people who seem to be standing or sitting by themselves. Approach the person with a smile, break the ice with a quick introduction and get going.

o   Approaching groups that are already engaged in a conversation may be a bit more difficult. Aim for smaller groups of two to four. Assess their approachability by observing the group formation in terms of the way people are standing. Let go of a group standing in a tight circle, engaged in deep conversation. It may be easier to break into a group where there are gaps in the way people are standing. Gather cues about the group's receptivity to a new entrant by observing the body language of people. Find a gap and walk up to a person who seems less engaged, introduce yourself and slip into the conversation.

o   Another way to get into the swing of the event is to have the host or the event organizer introduce you to a few people. Alternatively, walk up to the speaker and thank her for the talk, highlight the points you had noted, followed by a comment or a question. Or approach people who had asked questions during the question and answer session and weave a conversation around the talk and their question. Follow it up with an introduction.

o   While the idea is not to maximize the number of people you meet, it would be helpful to meet at least a few. If you are attending the event with your colleagues, try not to stick to them. Circulate around. After all, you are there to connect with people.

Follow-up—maintain your recall value.

Don't stop at just collecting business cards at an event. Write a follow-up email in the next 24 hours sharing your credentials. Connect on LinkedIn while the person still remembers you. Subsequently, adopt any of the easy ways described in Chapter 6 such as sharing relevant content, recommending a book or an event, engaging on the social media and greeting on festivals for keeping the connection active and establishing a recall value. But give it time. Don't rush into things.

- Focused more on their inner thoughts rather than social interactions, introverts work best in a quiet, minimally stimulating environment, while extroverts do better in a highly stimulating setting lined with social interactions like meetings, conversations and team activities.

- The difference is explained by the way their brains are wired. The neural pathways along which information is transmitted is longer in the brains of an introvert. As a result, introverts have to work harder to process external stimuli like loud noises and crowded events, which causes them discomfort.

- The nervous system of extroverts, on the other hand, is designed to expend energy as a result of which they constantly seek dopamine-enhancing stimuli like conversations, meetings and new experiences.

- Networking for introverts:
  - If large gatherings seem daunting, engage with smaller groups.

- o Rather than connecting face-to-face, explore alternative communication channels for networking like Twitter, LinkedIn or even calling people on phone.
- o It would be worthwhile trying to step out of your comfort zone and going to an event, after preparing adequately.

- Your networking toolkit
  - o Get your teeth into the event
    - Gather some information about the event in terms of the theme, organizers, speaker and people likely to be present in the audience.
  - o Set your goals
    - Figure out your objective in going to the event. It could be to learn, network, gain visibility or all these.
  - o Practise your introduction
    - Prepare an elevator pitch touching upon your organization, role and areas of expertise and interests. Remember that the introduction needs to be audience-centric and the same introduction will not work in every context.
  - o Prepare for small talk
    - Prepare some questions and talking points. These could be specific to people and their organization if you are planning to meet specific people at the event, general questions on the event or a range of current topics.
    - Listen intently. Don't worry too much about what you are going to say. Once you initiate a conversation with a question, listen intently for

both words and body language, and display your interest by smiling, nodding and commenting.

- o Approaching groups

  - – If you are alone and don't know anyone at the event, target people who are there by themselves. When approaching groups, target smaller groups of two to four. Assess the approachability of the group by observing the group formation and the body language of people.

- o Follow up

  - – Dash off an email sharing your credentials within a day of meeting someone at an event. Subsequently, keep the connection going by engaging on the social media, sharing content and greeting on festivals.

References

1. Cain S. Quiet: the power of introverts in a world that can't stop talking. New York: Crown Publishing Group; 2012.
2. Laney MO. The introvert advantage: how to thrive in an extrovert world. New York: Workman Publishing Company; 2002.
3. Baldoni J. Tips for making small talk with Bigwigs. Harv Bus Rev [Internet]. 22 March 2010. Available from: https://hbr.org/2010/03/tips-for-making-small-talk-wit
4. Harrell TW, Alpert B. Attributes of successful MBAs: a twenty-year longitudinal study. Stanford Graduate School of Business [Internet]. Available from: https://www.gsb.stanford.edu/faculty-research/working-papers/attributes-successful-mbas-twenty-year-longitudinal-study

Chapter 8

Making a Real Connection

The ability to engage with people and build constructive relationships is one of the mainstays of a strong brand. What goes into building these relationships? A warm disposition, affability and friendliness, propensity to appreciate and pay compliments and the ability to strike a conversation are some of the characteristics which predispose people positively towards you. Some of these have been discussed in the previous chapters. Outlined below are four skills or behaviours that could help you forge stronger relationships.

- Engaging with emotional intelligence

- Being a catalyst in people's growth

- Displaying vulnerability

- Understanding behavioural styles

Engaging with Emotional Intelligence

Ashima Shah, the delivery head at an IT company turned pale when she learnt that one of the critical applications of the company's most prestigious client had come to a grinding halt. Visions of losing a very remunerative project that was currently in the pipeline from the same client played havoc in her mind. Mustering all her courage, she picked up the phone to explain the situation to the client who was suitably incensed. She tried pacifying him by promising immediate action to assuage the situation and committed to calling back with an action plan before the end of the day.

Seething with rage, she sent for Sohail, the manager overseeing the application, and gave him a piece of her mind. He tried explaining but she would have none of it. She was just not ready to hear his side of the story, or excuses, as she called them. She had had enough of his inattention, incompetence and negligence! Tempers ran high and they engaged in a nasty exchange, before the manager marched out of the room exasperated, de-motivated and completely stressed out.

'People will forget what you said, people will forget what you did, but people will never forget how you made them feel,' was the astute observation of Maya Angelou, the famous American poet, memoirist, actress and civil rights activist. Sohail is unlikely to forget this incident in a hurry. The episode is likely to cast a shadow on their relationship and diminish Ashima's reputation, for organizations are social entities where word gets out fast and quick. She is likely to be perceived as one who's unable to exercise self-control and given to unleashing disruptive emotions oblivious of their corrosive impact on others.

Let's see how this episode could have alternatively played out.

As she put the phone down and fear gave way to anger, Ashima Shah sensed her heart pounding, temperature rising and a rush of adrenaline running through her body (self-awareness). She closed her eyes and took a few long, deep breaths. The extra dash of oxygen infused a sense of calm within her and helped her relax. She walked up to the water cooler and had a glass of cold water which further helped clear her thoughts, getting them back to focus on the solution (self-management).

She realized that there were two issues at hand that had to be dealt with—first, and the more immediate and critical one was to get the client's application up on its feet; and the second was to address Sohail's performance shortfall. She realized that it would be best to delink the two. Having worked this out in her mind, she sent for Sohail and explained the situation to him. Rather than playing a blame game, she engaged him in a productive, solution-oriented discussion, and together they worked out an action plan to set the application running. Once that was implemented and the client placated, she set up another meeting with Sohail a couple of days later to share her observations and concerns about his performance. She took care to be objective and non-judgmental, both in her choice of words as well as her mannerisms, knowing that any other approach could turn him defensive and provoke unnecessary debate (empathy). The conversation concluded with Sohail committing to an action plan to address his developmental areas and thanked Shah for supporting him (relationship-management).

This time around, Shah had engaged with emotional intelligence, leveraging its four critical pillars—*self-awareness, self-management, social awareness or empathy and relationship management.*

In his 1996 bestseller *Emotional Intelligence,* Daniel Goleman[1] described emotional intelligence as the ability to accurately per-ceive and manage your own emotions and understand and navigate through those of others, thus enhancing your capacity to influence people, manage conflicts, lead others and build relationships. He argued that cognitive skills like decision-making, problem-solving and logical reasoning are entry-level skills for success. What really propels you forward is your ability to understand people, connect with them and take them along. In a study done by TalentSmart,[2] a premier provider of emotional intelligence-related products and services, it was found that emotional intelligence was a stronger predictor of performance, when juxtaposed with 33 other important workplace skills and explained 58 per cent of success in all types of jobs. Another survey by TalentSmart found that 90 per cent of top performers were also high on emotional intelligence, whereas 80 per cent of the bottom performers were low on emotional intelligence, indicating a strong, positive correlation between emotional intelligence and performance.

Emotional Intelligence in Action

Born in Tuticorin in South India, Archana Patchirajan[3] moved to New York in 2002. She went on to become a serial entrepreneur after a successful career at Wall Street firms. She founded her first start-up, MyCityWay, in 2010 after winning the NYC BigApps competition (an annual competition that provides developers, entrepreneurs and designers a platform to build technological products that address the civic issues affecting New York City). Subsequently, she co-founded Hubbl, a business-to-business application distribution and discovery platform.

At one point, when pushed to the wall at Hubbl, Patchirajan was compelled to call her 25-member team of high calibre, experienced engineers, who worked out of India, to inform them that she would have to let them go. This drastic step was triggered by the company's inability to pay salaries when the initial seed funding had dried up. To her amazement, however, the team displayed incredible faith in Patchirajan's vision and leadership by choosing to stay back and continue working with a voluntary salary cut to help the company tide over the difficult phase. Their conviction paid off a few years later when, in 2013, Airpush, the mobile ad network, bought up Hubbl for $15 million, heralding happy times for everyone.

What did Patchirajan do to elicit this extraordinary response from her team? What does it say about her brand? Her brand, clearly, speaks of exceptional people skills and a high degree of emotional intelligence. This was corroborated by one of her team members who mentioned that when things would go wrong, Patchirajan would always give them space to fix the situation and learn from it, without losing her cool. Her ability to manage difficult situations through a generous dollop of emotional intelligence, along with other good people practices like treating people with respect and building constructive relationships had led her team to support and stay on in Hubbl despite a shortfall in compensation. Dealing with people through emotional intelligence, thus, comes across as the cornerstone of Patchirajan's brand.

Empathy and Self-regulation

Aryan was an executive in the operations team of an e-commerce company. Stretched to the brim and working on tight timelines during the COVID-19 lockdown, he erroneously sent the rate file, instead of the product file, to an external partner. When the magnitude of his error dawned on him, he realized that what he had done was indeed suicidal. What will his manager say? Extremely stressed out, he wrote an email to his manager, Manav, apologizing for his indiscretion. But guess what? Manav responded saying, 'No problem. Let's move ahead.'

It is easy to fly off the handle in a scenario laden with organizational restructuring, job and salary cuts, physical stress emanating from the constant use of technology, along with the added burden of domestic chores. But by successfully managing his emotions, Manav demonstrated a high degree of emotional intelligence, which not only motivated his team member but also added the label of 'calmness personified' to his brand.

Being a Catalyst

Agitated and stressed Kavita, an HR business partner in a prominent real estate company, was ready to hit the roof. The business head had given her a two-day deadline to complete the competition mapping exercise which entailed the arduous process of tapping into her industry network and talking to people to gather market intelligence. 'How unreasonable!' she thought. 'How can he expect me to complete this exercise in such a short period, given that the performance management cycle is in full swing? And to think that he is blatantly overstepping the performance appraisal timelines himself!' she exclaimed to herself. Then her thoughts veered towards the disciplinary issue in her constituency that needed attention, plus the candidates she had to line up for interviews.

Overwhelmed, she stormed into the HR head, Rakesh Sondi's office, requesting him to negotiate the timelines with the business head and also seeking some time concessions on the HR assignments that she was slated to turn in that week.

In a bid to calm her down, Sondi first offered her a glass of water and asked after her kids and her prized potted plants that she was so proud of. Then he gently drew her into a dialogue encouraging her to think through all her deliverables and prioritize them based on their importance and urgency from the stakeholders' perspective. He also got her to think about ways she could engage with her stakeholders to negotiate timelines. He then proceeded to put some colour around the grim market conditions, which had caused sales to plummet, putting the business head under tremendous pressure. The competition mapping data was critical for his impending meeting with the chairman later that week. Having understood the big picture, she was now able to empathize instead of getting exasperated with the business head.

She felt a sense of relief as she walked out of Sondi's cabin. Thinking back on their conversation, she realized that he had neither allowed her any time concessions, nor given her any solution on a platter. He had, in fact, just listened intently, shared some facts and asked a few pertinent questions, which helped her put things in perspective, explore options and prioritise her tasks. He had given her space to unravel the answers herself. As she got clarity on her next course of action during their 45-minute conversation, distress and anxiety slowly ebbed, giving way to composure and confidence. She felt energized and more in control of things.

This interaction helped reinforce their rapport, as Kavita's regard for Sondi went up several notches higher. It also helped Sondi strengthen his brand by reinforcing his reputation of being an enabler, a good listener and a remarkable mentor.

Displaying Vulnerability

Do you tend to portray the best side of yourself, the positive, attractive and successful side, when engaging with others? Is this always the best strategy to connect with people? Not always, according to the research of Arthur Aron,[4] professor of psychology at the State University of New York at Stony Brook.

Professor Aron and his team of researchers had conducted an experiment with a group of students, where the students were put into two cohorts and encouraged to engage in conversation in groups of two. The researchers guided the conversation through a set of questions or talking points that they shared with the participants. The talking points handed out to the first group revolved around small-talk topics like your favourite restaurant, your last holiday, your most memorable movie and the like. The talking points shared with the second group, on the other hand, started with similar small-talk topics but gradually moved to deeper topics such as 'talk about the time you experienced failure', 'when was the last time you cried' and 'whose death are you most likely to be affected by'.

45 minutes into the experiment, the participants were asked to rate their level of comfort with their partner and how connected they felt with each other. The level of intimacy and closeness derived as a result of this conversation by groups in the second cohort was far higher than what was reported by their counterparts in the first cohort. This interaction, in fact, even triggered some long-term friendships among people in the second cohort.

Professor Aron and his team, therefore, concluded that disclosing your whole, not just your perfect self, including your highs and lows and your triumphs and failures portrays you as human, someone who is fallible and vulnerable and whom one need not be in awe of. Such a person is easier to connect with, easier to establish stronger bonds and forge deeper relationships with.

Arvind Charanyan V., a senior leader at a fashion and lifestyle e-commerce portal, agrees. 'I have found that revealing your whole self to people, including your vulnerabilities and imperfections, your wins and losses renders you more authentic and genuine. People then find it easier to relate to you,' he says.

Owning Up

Sharing one of his career experiences, Arvind said that a successful launch of a brand or a product on an online portal is a function of a constellation of factors. One of the most critical of these is a highly accurate projection of demand. 'On one occasion, I went horribly wrong with my projection for a new brand that we were launching and was extremely disappointed with myself. I knew that my credibility with my stakeholders was at stake. I thought hard, debriefed on the situation and chose to own up my error of judgment before my team and superiors. I explained the discrepancy in my estimation and the lessons I had learnt. I stand enriched from this experience having learnt some valuable lessons the hard way. I often share this experience with different teams that I have been called upon to lead, in the process sending out the message that it is okay to fail as long as you learn from it,' says Arvind.

Seeking Feedback: The Key to Improvement

Seeking and embracing feedback is another dimension of vulnerability. 'I have come a long way since my Unilever days when I was naive enough to disregard other people's perception about me as irrelevant. Now I see merit in understanding how my stakeholders perceive me because that's their reality, and have adopted the practice of regularly soliciting feedback both from my superiors as well as my team,' says Arvind.

Sharing another experience in his career, when he had moved into a new role, Arvind says 'In a bid to understand the new business, I set out getting my hands dirty by getting involved in all the finer details of business. I was also seeking to establish a rapport with my new team which was very closely knit and had shared a great bond with my predecessors. I decided to invest time engaging with them one on one, soliciting feedback about my management style and understanding what I could do to make things better for them. To my surprise, I received very candid and unequivocal comments like, 'we don't feel trusted', 'we feel that we are being micromanaged' and so forth.'

'Their responses were very informative and insightful. I took the approach of filtering out the stuff that I thought was not so relevant, while actively working on what I thought was really pertinent. I took the time to explain to them as to why I was doing what I was doing. I was getting down to the nitty-gritty, not with the intention of micromanaging, but to learn and come up to speed with understanding the business.

I worked on the feedback and at the same time remained steadfast on things which I felt were non-negotiable. A few months later, I went back to the team and shared the actions that I had taken in response to their feedback. This act of standing vulnerable before them went a long way in helping me move a few steps forward into being accepted in the team. Starting off at 1, on a scale of 1 to 10, I think I have now graduated to a 6. I still have a long way to go, I know,' said Arvind, with a smile.

Sharing Your Setbacks

Chetna Vasishth, who runs ChetChat, a chat show in the career and education space, came across as very genuine when she shared her vulnerability saying, 'Two years and 95 videos later, I had almost reached a breaking point. I was ready to give up as my channel was languishing with zero inflow of revenue. But I caved in to my husband's persuasive argument encouraging me to hit a century before wrapping up finally. And then, in my penultimate episode, I interviewed R. Satya Narayanan, CEO, Career Launcher Ltd, who, sensing my disenchantment, showed me the big picture and urged me to hang on. Edu-tech, he said, was slated to be the next big thing. I heard him out, not entirely convinced. Then came my hundredth and the last episode, which turned out to be a resounding success, giving me the strength and conviction to continue.'

Disclosing a Failure

A participant from a global investment bank at one of my leadership programs took me quite by surprise by his unflinching narration of one of the darkest moments of his life—failure in class 12 exam. His vivid description of loss of confidence and credibility, and his inability to face family, friends and classmates, touched a chord in me. At one point, he had even contemplated suicide, he said. Today, of course, he is a super successful senior leader in the industry.

It is certainly courageous to make a disclosure like this, as it would be so much easier to simply keep failure under the wraps. He rose several notches higher in my esteem and his brand became concomitant with daring and courage. More importantly, it helped us establish a rapport.

Understanding Behavioural Styles

People are wired differently. For instance, some are friendly and others reserved, some people-oriented while others task-oriented, some make quick decisions and others need time to ponder, some are up for anything exciting, while others prefer the predictability of the status quo. Any mismatch or misalignment of behavioural styles can trigger noise, impeding communication and impacting interpersonal relations.

Read the dialogue between a customer and a storekeeper in Scenario 8.1 and assess their behavioural styles.

Scenario 8.1

Storekeeper	How can I help you?
Customer	*(enthusiastically, with a big smile)* Good morning! How are you doing? I am looking for a book called *TED Talks: The Official TED Guide to Public Speaking* by Chris Anderson. I believe this is one of the most insightful books ever written on public speaking. One of my friends had recommended this book saying that it had helped her hone her presentation skills immensely!
Storekeeper	*(looking at his watch)* Who's the publisher?
Customer	I am not sure but let me Google it for you.
	(Settles down in a chair, pulls out his phone and starts scanning the internet to identify the publisher.

Looks up to say 'hi' to another customer who has just walked in.)

Storekeeper   *(Impatiently)* Well, we have the book in the store. It costs ₹533. Why don't you settle the bill while I go and get the book? I will be back in exactly three minutes.

Customer   Sure, let me walk up to the coffee machine and get a cup of coffee while you are gone.

Storekeeper   I suggest that you make the payment first. With so many customers walking in, the queue at the cash counter is just getting longer.

Customer   Sure, I'll do that.

Clearly, the customer is friendly, talkative and enthusiastic, whereas the storekeeper is reticent and reserved. This seemingly unfriendly disposition of the storekeeper may put the customer off, who may decide to try another bookstore the next time around. The storekeeper, on the other hand, may have been annoyed by the customer's verbosity and overfriendly manner. Thus, while the task was achieved, the interaction per se fell somewhat short of gratification from the perspective of both the customer and the storekeeper. But this need not have been so.

Let's see how this could have played out alternatively. Read Scenario 8.2.

Scenario 8.2

Storekeeper   How can I help you?

Customer   *(enthusiastically, with a big smile)* Good morning! How are you doing? I am looking for a book called *TED Talks: The Official TED Guide to Public Speaking* by Chris Anderson. I believe this is one of the most

Storekeeper	Oh! Really? Sounds interesting! I think I should make time to read the book as well. By the way, do you know who the publisher is?
Customer	I am not sure but let me Google it for you.
Storekeeper	No, no, don't worry! I will check it out.
	In fact, I have found the book. It costs ₹533. Would you like to settle the bill while I go and get the book for you?
Customer	Sure, let me walk up to the coffee machine and get a cup of coffee while you are gone.
Clerk	Sure! The coffee machine is located at the corner next to the staircase.
Customer	Thank you!

insightful books ever written on public speaking. One of my friends had recommended this book saying that it had helped her hone her presentation skills immensely!

This time, the storekeeper adapted his behavioural style, aligning it with that of the customer rendering their interaction far more effective. This adaptation calls for an awareness towards your own behavioural tendencies, an observant eye to gauge the behaviour of others and then flexing of your style to match that of the other person for better communication and conflict resolution and for gaining endorsement and striking better relationships.

Read Scenarios 8.3 and 8.4.

Scenario 8.3

| Executive | Around 30 per cent of the complaints this month have emanated from late deliveries. |
| Manager | What do you mean 'about 30 per cent'? Is it 29 per cent or 31 per cent? |

Executive	31.35 per cent of the complaints this month have emanated from late deliveries.
Manager	Around 30 per cent, right?

Had the executive in Scenario 8.3 known about the manager's proclivity for precision, he could have obviated this dialogue by furnishing a precise number to the last decimal point.

Similarly, in Scenario 8.4, instead of stating a precise number to the last decimal place, the executive could have rounded it off, thus addressing the manager's preference for approximation and big picture.

Scenario 8.5

Suraj is the sales manager at a polyester filament yarn-manufacturing company. An extrovert, Suraj likes to interact with people and has the ability to engage in a conversation with almost everyone. He is informal and intuitive, likes to adopt new approaches to work and works best in an unstructured environment.

Sara Textile Mills, one of his client companies for many years, has hired a new procurement manager, Sunder. Sunder is formal and business-like, not inclined towards making small talk. He tends to get into detailed discussions, preferring to clarify and reconfirm every point. Reviewing data from a number of different angles, he always asks for more, thereby slowing down the decision-making process. He is a perfectionist with a keen eye for gaps and inaccuracies. Very structured in his approach, on one occasion, he refused to attend a meeting since he had not received the agenda and the calendar invite on time.

While Suraj found Sunder to be demanding, impatient and unfriendly, Sunder experienced his meetings with Suraj frustrating and inefficient.

From the above narration, it is apparent that Suraj is people-oriented, informal and unstructured, while Sunder is task-oriented, formal and organized with a proclivity for data. The obvious misalignment in their working styles is obstructing the effectiveness of their interactions, causing some disturbance and discomfort in their relationship.

The Four Behavioural Styles

Dr William Moulton Marston was a writer and psychologist with three degrees from Harvard University. He was the first to propound a framework, categorizing people into four quadrants based on their behavioural patterns, when he published his book *Emotions of Normal People* in 1928. While the framework has evolved over time, the fundamental principles have remained unchanged.

Four behavioural styles emerge at the crossroads of two parameters:

- Task versus people orientation
- Degree of introversion versus extroversion.

Note that far from being binary, different shades of grey run in a continuum along these parameters.

Given below is a brief description of the four behavioural styles.

Dominant

Competitive, tenacious, independent and result-oriented with a concern for *what's* being done, rather than *how* it is done, the dominant is up for challenges, has an appetite for risk and an

Figure 8.1. The Behavioural Style Grid

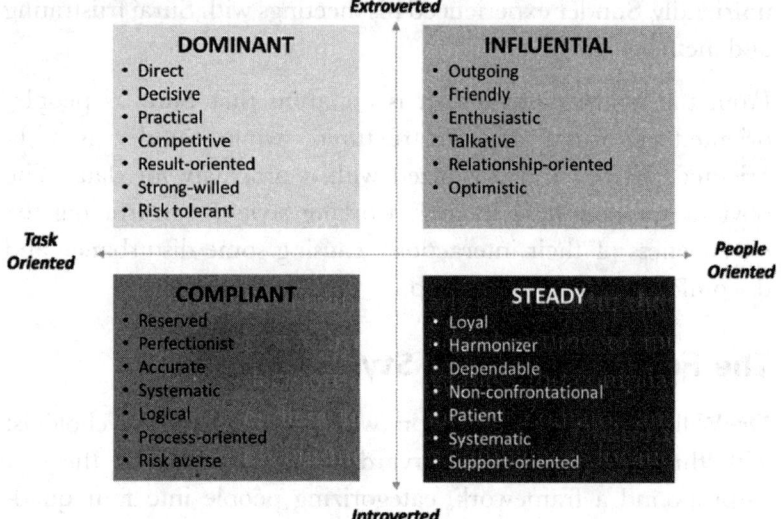

Source: Adapted from William Moulton Marston's model of behaviour.

inherent need to lead. A person characterized by this style is decisive, practical and organized. More task than relationship-oriented, the dominant is direct in their communication, never hesitating to call a spade a spade.

Influential

Friendly, talkative, enthusiastic, optimistic and socially adept, the influential has an inherent need for social affiliation and is game for anything new and exciting. An influential thrives in the spotlight and tends to motivate and encourage others.

Steady

Friendly, supportive, dependable and a good listener, the steady gets along well with people and works towards building long-term relationships. They are often referred to as harmonizers for their stabilizing effect on people. Patient and hardworking, the steady sees a task to completion, avoids confrontation and performs best in a stable and predictable environment.

Compliant

The compliant is reserved, task rather than relationship-oriented and a perfectionist with a proclivity for accuracy and precision. Systematic, orderly and logical, the compliant goes by the rules, is risk averse and takes time to mull over facts before making decisions. For instance, the compliant can be expected to spend endless hours surfing Zomato, analysing restaurants in terms of cuisine, rates, ambience, location and parking space when planning a family dinner.

Two points are worth noting about this framework. First, behavioural styles are based purely on observable behaviour and have little to do with the person's inner qualities, values, attitude and aptitude that lie deep within. Second, each person embodies a behavioural style that is a unique blend of all the four styles, with a preference for one or two styles that are displayed more often. These constitute the person's primary and secondary styles respectively.

It is important, thus, to introspect and heighten awareness towards one's own behavioural style, be a keen observer of people, their mannerisms and behavioural patterns, and be open to flexing ones style, aligning it with that of the other person for better interactions and relationships. Moreover, rather than trying to slot people into a specific style, it would be far more useful to watch out for and discern different elements of behaviour and think about the best way of dealing with it.

CALL FOR ACTION

Quiz: Understanding Behavioural Styles

1. Which behavioural style prioritizes these?

   a. Ensuring accuracy

   b. Engaging with people

   c. Providing support

   d. Taking up a challenge

2. With which behavioural style would you associate these?

   a. Independence

   b. Popularity

   c. Group acceptance

   d. Correctness

3. Which behavioural style values these?

   a. Loyalty

   b. Results

   c. Quality

   d. Freedom of expression

4. Which behavioural style is associated with these needs?

   a. Recognition

   b. Accuracy

   c. Harmony

   d. Concrete results

5. Which behavioural style may have the following limitations?

    a.   Lack of concern for others

    b.   Indecision

    c.   Being over-critical

    d.   Impulsiveness

Four ways of expanding and strengthening your relationships are:

- **Engaging with emotional intelligence**

  Emotional intelligence refers to your ability to accurately identify, understand and manage your own emotions and understand and navigate through those of others; thus enhancing your capability for striking better relationships, resolving conflicts and influencing people. Emotional intelligence thus stands on four critical pillars—self-awareness, self-management, social awareness and relationship management.

  Studies point to a strong positive correlation between emotional intelligence and professional success. Further, as you move up the hierarchy, emotional intelligence plays an increasingly vital role to succeed on the progressively expansive turf that you are called to play upon, and the far more complex set of relationships you are required to manage.

- **Catalysing people's development**

  People look up to those who support their growth by providing feedback and advice, and nudge them in the right direction; while the person who catalyses the growth benefits from sharpening his/her people development skills, building a reputation for shaping and nurturing people and the satisfaction of being instrumental in someone's progress. These mutually beneficial engagements draw people into closer relationships.

- **Displaying vulnerability**

  By revealing not just your perfect side but your whole self, including your failures and setbacks, you come across as more human, an individual who is not infallible and, therefore, easier to relate to. This helps establish stronger bonds and forge deeper relationships.

- **Understanding behavioural styles**

  People are wired differently in terms of their behaviour patterns. Dr William Moulton Marston had propounded a framework categorizing people based on their behaviour into four quadrants—dominant, influential, steady and compliant.

  A mismatch or misalignment of behavioural styles can cause irritants that can strain relationships. It is important, therefore, to be aware of your own behavioural style and be able to discern that of others and adapt your style in order to render your relationships more effective.

References

1. Goleman D. Emotional intelligence: why it can matter more than IQ. New York: Bantam Books; 1995.
2. TalentSmart [Internet]. About emotional intelligence. Available from: https://www.talentsmart.com/about/emotional-intelligence.php
3. Seppälä E. What bosses gain by being vulnerable. Harv Bus Rev [Internet]. 11 Dec 2014. Available from: https://hbr.org/2014/12/what-bosses-gain-by-being-vulnerable
4. Aron A, Melinat E, Aron E, Vallone RD, Bator RJ. The experimental generation of interpersonal closeness: a procedure and some preliminary findings. Pers Soc Psychol Bull [Internet]. Available from: https://psychodramaaustralia.edu.au/sites/default/files/falling_in_love-aron.pdf

04

Visibility

The Third Dimension

Chapter 9

Promoting Yourself without Seeming to

Sunset at Montmajour is a stunning landscape painted by one the most celebrated Dutch artists of the 19th century, Vincent Van Gough, in 1888 (see Figure 9.1). For most part of its life, branded as a fake, this painting lay unrecognized, uncelebrated and unloved, dumped in the attic of the home of Christian Nicolai

Figure 9.1. Sunset at Montmajour by Vincent Van Gough

Source: https://en.wikipedia.org/wiki/Sunset_at_Montmajour#/media/File:Sunset_at_Montmajour_1888_Van_Gogh.jpg

Mustad, a Norwegian industrialist. In 2013, after a comprehensive investigation process that lasted over two years, it was finally recognized as an authentic Van Gough painting and acclaimed as a masterpiece. It was unveiled in Amsterdam's Van Gough museum and Axel Rüger, the museum's director, claimed that 'the painting is absolutely sensational, a once in a lifetime experience.'

What does this story reveal?

An object may have intrinsic value, but it may not be recognized and appreciated unless it is polished and presented in the right forum. After all, with all its inherent value, how good is an invaluable pearl that sits on the seabed? It is acknowledged and appreciated only after it is retrieved, refined, furbished and exhibited to the right audience.

Interestingly, what holds for an object also holds for a person!

Jeffrey Pfeffer, Professor of organizational behaviour at the Graduate School of Business, Stanford University, has categorically stated in his book *Power: Why Some People Have It—and Others Don't* that performance alone does not guarantee success. In other words, just excelling at work and delivering on your key result areas is not enough to propel your career forward. The message of your performance and accomplishments needs to get across to your stakeholders—people who make decisions about you and your career. Unless they know about your unique strengths and contribution, how will they give you credit for it in terms of a promotion, challenging assignments and increased job responsibilities?

Clearly, it is not enough to be the best. It is just as important to be perceived as being the best by your stakeholders.

Companies spend a whopping 11.2% of their annual revenue, on an average, on overall marketing.[1] This was the finding of the

Chief Marketing Officer Spend Survey conducted by Gartner in 2018–2019, covering 621 marketing executives in North America and the UK at companies with an annual revenue ranging from $500 million to $10 billion. Now that's big money! Evidently, there's a high positive correlation between marketing and promotional effort and the overall revenue growth. Just as organizations find value in marketing and promoting their products and services for generating awareness and visibility, individuals too stand to benefit from the right strategy for communicating their strengths, achievements and the value they bring to the table.

A personal brand thus needs to be promoted for it to gain visibility and recognition amongst stakeholders. This section will provide tools and techniques for promoting your brand responsibly, without sounding like you are blowing your own trumpet.

Self-promotion Feels Uncomfortable

What emotion does the thought of promoting yourself evoke? 'Squeamish' and 'uncomfortable' are the most common responses I have heard from the thousands of people I have posed this question to. Conjuring up the image of blowing one's own trumpet, the idea of self-promotion instils a feeling of awkwardness, something that doesn't feel quite right. It goes against the value of modesty that's been culturally infused in us. 'Work without a reward in mind. Do your duty, but don't concern yourself with the results,' was Lord Krishna's famous and oft-quoted advice to Arjuna on the battlefield of Kurukshetra, which is at the heart of the Bhagavad Gita.

So, the starting point really is to rethink and reframe the idea of self-promotion. What is self-promotion and what it is not?

Redefine Self-promotion

Think of a product first. What message is the marketer communicating when they promote a packet of biscuits? The obvious answer is: They're drawing attention to the product by building awareness and sensitizing people to its key benefits with the objective of influencing purchase decisions. Now let's apply the same principle to an individual. Self-promotion is about calling attention to your key strengths, competencies and achievements, by communicating these to people who can leverage the information for making better decisions. So, the key point is that the communication is mutually beneficial, since it is as much about the individual as it is about the people it is being communicated to. Consider the example below.

Rahul is managing a high profile, time-sensitive project for a prestigious client in a global IT company. He manages nine people and typically runs a 12-hour day. Currently, all his energies are focused on ensuring a timely project delivery. The appraisal season is just around the corner and he is worrying about how he would do justice to the performance review of his team. How would he do a good job of mapping his team to the infamous bell curve, especially as four of his high-performing team members appear to be at par in terms of their performance on all the key parameters. While Rahul is completely in the know about their performance on the big-ticket items, the differentiation probably lies in some of the smaller things they did on the job, which Rahul has not had the time or the bandwidth to observe.

Rhea, one of his team members, who works at the client's site, had recently faced a difficult situation when the client came up with a request that lay beyond the defined realm of the project. Rhea thought hard, came up with an alternate solution and dexterously positioned it as a win-win approach. The client was convinced, and he accepted the solution with a smile. Rhea thus resolved the issue at her level and pre-empted an escalation to her manager, thus saving him time and worry. Rahul would have never learnt about Rhea's ability to handle issues independently, her initiative and persuasion skills, let alone give her credit for these, had she not shared this episode at one of the team meetings. Rahul made a mental note of it and secretly thanked Rhea for sharing details and providing him some solid inputs for the impending appraisal.

Rhea had, in effect, promoted herself. But the vital point is that this communication had benefitted her manager as much as it had helped Rhea gain visibility. Therefore, positioning self-promotion as a mutually beneficial communication eradicates the shadow of 'tooting your horn'. So, take the 'self' out of self-promotion, and reframe it in your mind as 'being not just about me, but about us'.

Having said that, self-promotion is a delicate activity. Overdo it and you come across as a braggadocio, and shun the limelight and you may deprive yourself of accolades that are concomitant with it. Self-promotion, therefore, should be subtle, measured and understated.

Clothe Your Self-promotion in Anecdotes

I have been writing for over 10 years and have more than 55 published articles on leadership, professional skills and diversity in some of the leading Indian newspapers. Nothing has contributed to building my brand as much as writing has. In the early days, each time my article was published, I would cut it out, file it away carefully and feel good about it. And nobody beyond my family and immediate team at work would learn about it.

But later, I started the practice of sharing my published articles with people in my network—current and potential clients, business associates, friends, acquaintances and family. This not only helped me position myself as a subject-matter expert, but also contributed to my brand recall. But writing has not come easy to me. All through my formative years, I remember having struggled with essays, frequently falling short of both words and ideas. Even today, when I look upon a piece of my writing, I wonder whether it is actually my work! It has been a slow, arduous journey, entailing a lot of sweat and hard work. So, the point is that if I could do it, I am confident that there are a lot of others whose talent is just waiting to be discovered. I would strongly advocate people to unravel their writing talent and leverage it to enhance their personal brand.

What did I just do? I promoted my talent and achievement by relating a story around it, and probably this did not come across as bragging or tooting my horn for three reasons—first, there was an element of humility because I spoke about an achievement as well as the related challenges in the same breath; second, I just stated facts, leaving the evaluation to the reader; third, the communication was contextual since we are discussing the concept of self-promotion and the reader is likely to be looking for insights and examples of ways to promote oneself effectively.

A software engineer, Neena was striving to write an algorithm to solve a particularly complex problem. Burning the midnight lamp, she had tried six different approaches but none had given her the desired result. Finally, frustrated, she called Aryan, her colleague from a previous organization she had worked with. She had lost touch with Aryan but had an opportunity to renew her association when she met him at a recently held conference. Aryan helped her with a crucial clue that enabled her to crack the algorithm. She, thus, succeeded in running a particular process with greater efficiency, saving 20 seconds on each run. It had been a challenging, laborious and an enriching experience.

Neena was hesitant to share this experience with her team thinking that 'it's not a big deal!' But when she presented the algorithm and shared the story outlining the challenges she had faced, the different approaches that she tried, what had worked and what had not and finally how she had obtained the final clue from her network, people listened with interest.

Research shows that by igniting multiple spots in the brain of the listener, stories tend to be far more appealing and memorable than a mere statement of facts. More importantly, the team benefitted from Neena's story as they were able to take a page from her work and apply it in their own space without having to reinvent the wheel; her manager learnt about Neena's networking and problem-solving skills; and finally, Neena benefitted too, as she was acknowledged and commended for her work.

Therefore, weave a story around a problem that you had encountered and the smart thinking and hard work it took to resolve it, lacing it with real-life characters, suspense and drama, and most importantly, making it relevant to the audience. Ensure that the audience has a learning or a take-away from your experience.

Communicate Your Ideas

The Game Theory

John Forbes Nash Jr, an American mathematician, won the Nobel prize for Economics in 1994 for his seminal work on the mathematics of game theory. *A Beautiful Mind*, a biographical movie on Nash's life, directed by Ron Howard, based on Sylvia Nasar's bestselling, Pulitzer Prize-nominated book of the same name, depicts how Nash conceived the idea of the game theory.

In one of the scenes in the movie, Nash and his friends, engaged in a friendly banter at a pub, are eyeballing a group of girls that has just entered the pub. All of them are taken in by one particular girl, a blonde, and as they compete with each other to get her attention, one of the boys echoes the father of modern economics, Adam Smith's famous principle—'in competition, individual ambition serves the common good.' This triggers a thought in Nash, who, finding his eureka moment, challenges Adam Smith's principle that had been revered as the gospel truth for over a 100 years. 'Adam Smith needs revision. The best results come when everyone in the group does what is best for him and for the group,' he announces. Thanking the blonde, he runs out of the pub and develops and refines this theory over the next few months.

He then presents his theory to his professor, who is taken aback by his audacity to challenge something that had been propounded by Adam Smith and had been held sacrosanct for more than a century, but appreciates and commends the idea nevertheless.

By presenting a bold idea that challenged a widely prevalent belief, Nash not only promoted himself but also built a reputation of being audacious, confident, risk-taker and an out-of-the-box thinker, with these descriptors getting firmly entrenched in his brand.

Thus, having the courage to express your ideas, no matter how outlandish, is an effective way of self-promotion.

Who Comes First?

'Employees first, customers second' is the radical, path-breaking idea propounded by Vineet Nayar, the former CEO of HCL Technologies. Nayar proposes that for any organization striving to create a unique and differential value for its customers, it is imperative to focus on the 'value zone', or the critical interface of employees and customers, where value really gets created. He presents a compelling story of the implementation of this idea at HCL Technologies which led to its dramatic turnaround in the mid-1990s.

Implicit in the idea 'employees first, customers second' is a strategy that circumvents conventional management practices and turns the organizational structure over, to create a culture of transparency and mutual accountability between the employees and the management. How was this achieved at HCL Technologies?

The leaders led the way by walking the talk to establish their credibility. The enabling functions like HR, administration and

IT were held accountable to the employees, by enabling employee to open a 'Trouble Ticket' whenever faced with a service-related issue. The concerned department was required to close the ticket within the stipulated turnaround time. Similarly, the practice of 360-degree reviews was initiated wherein anybody could give feedback to anyone, including the CEO and the management team, and the feedback results were published on the website. In the spirit of transparency, the company's financial results were shared with the employees to enable them to see where the company and particularly their department stood in terms of performance. And during the 2008 financial meltdown, when large-scale layoffs were being staged elsewhere, at HCL Technologies, the management was actually collaborating with the employees, soliciting their ideas for dealing with the difficult situation at hand, thereby creating an environment marked by energy, enthusiasm and ownership.

Thus, by implementing this philosophy, not only did Nayar propel HCL Technologies into the most influential IT services companies club, he also established his brand as a thinker and a thought leader and gained immense visibility by virtue of presenting his idea in the form of a book, which has received widespread acclaim and has sold more than 100,000 copies.

Present Ideas That May Not Be Your Own

'The world is flat.' Who do you associate this concept with? Thomas L. Friedman, of course!

Friedman is an internationally renowned reporter, columnist, the recipient of three Pulitzer Prizes and the author of six bestselling books. In his fourth book, *The World is Flat: A Brief History of the 21st Century* published in 2005, he describes how technology has brought about a seismic change and revolutionized the way work is done globally. Instant communication, freer flow of information and speedy travel have led to a level playing field, enabling countries like India and China to become an integral part of the global supply chain for manufacturing and service industries. The world would do well to adapt and adjust to this new reality.

But was this originally Friedman's idea? No.

In an article in *New York Times Magazine*,[2] Friedman talks about how he chanced upon the idea of the world being flat on his visit to Infosys Ltd, one of the largest Indian IT services companies, at Bangalore in the context of a documentary film on 'outsourcing' that he was doing for the Discovery Times channel. Nandan Nilekani, the then CEO of Infosys, had walked him to their global video-conference room and proudly explained how easy it was for them to connect with all the key players from their global supply chain for any project through virtual meetings. He went on to explain that the massive investment in technology, broadband connectivity, fall in computer prices, explosion of email software and search engines like Google had created a platform which made it possible to slice and dice any piece of intellectual work and deliver it from multiple locations across the globe. He summed up the discussion saying, 'Tom, the playing field is being levelled.' This phrase resonated with Friedman and stuck in his mind.

He played with the phrase and reworded it as 'the world is flat'. This tagline is now synonymous with Thomas Friedman, not Nandan Nilekani. This idea is the central theme of his book *The World is Flat*, which became the number 1 *The New York Times* bestseller and received the Goldman Sachs/Financial Times Book of the Year Award.

Friedman was applauded for an idea that was sculpted, developed and polished by him and, more importantly, presented to the world in the form of a book.

Thus, having a compelling idea alone is not enough. The idea needs to be presented and promoted to the right audience using the right channels to gain visibility, recognition and applause.

Moreover, the idea need not necessarily be yours. But it is important to stay within the bounds of ethics by acknowledging and giving credit to the person whose idea you are taking forward. As did Friedman.

Go beyond Your Role

Armed with five degrees in mechanical engineering and economics, German born Klaus Schwab started his academic career as a business professor at the University of Geneva. However, rather than just sticking to academic pursuits, Schwab demonstrated great vision when he launched the European Management Symposium in 1971, providing a forum for business, academic and political leaders to engage and exchange ideas. 450 delegates, including the CEOs of the top corporations of Europe and 50 faculty from the world's most renowned universities, attended the Symposium at Davos, a ski resort in the Swiss Alps.

Based on the overwhelming success of the first conference, this became an annual event, and in 1987, the title of the forum was changed to World Economic Forum to align it with its expanding scope. The roster of the participants and speakers also expanded to include politicians, industry honchos, academicians, heads of states, technology czars, climate activists, movie stars, non-profit organizations and philanthropists who meet annually to discuss and brainstorm around major global political and economic issues, new ideas, the latest trends and developments in a range of different fields.

By moving beyond academics and by conceiving, executing and promoting the idea of a global forum, Klaus Schwab distinguished himself and catapulted his brand to a very different level. As the chief of the World Economic Forum, even today, he is actively involved in determining the themes and identifying the participant list of this very exclusive forum.

Within a year of joining an insurance company, Meghna Rathi, a customer experience manager, built a reputation of being an expert in her field, as well as someone who is always up for tasks beyond her role. For instance, Meghna put her hand up when the marketing head was looking for someone to drive the company's marketing awards event. As the organizing committee lead, she spent endless hours coordinating with different stakeholders to identify the award categories, the judges, the chief guest and the event flow. This not only gave her visibility but also an opportunity to engage and build connections with people beyond her department and with people outside the company.

Similarly, she was at the forefront of the marketing quiz, which turned out to be a thumping success, again giving an opportunity to get in front of an organization-wide audience. On another occasion, when the CEO needed a representative from the marketing department for the new product development committee, again Meghna volunteered, and this proved to be a great opportunity for her to gain visibility with the CEO.

Shortly thereafter, she was invited by the sales department for their annual sales conference. She went for the conference despite her boss's tepid response. Listening carefully to the various presentations during the conference, she was able to identify areas where marketing could help sales. For instance, since she had access to comprehensive customer-related data, she offered to curate data around customer behaviour which could help sales. True to her word, she shared a very relevant dashboard with sales soon after the conference. The sales group found it extremely helpful and, soon after, the national sales head invited her for a discussion on how the dashboard could be further fine-tuned. Suddenly, she became the go-to person in marketing for the sales group.

Meghna became highly visible with different stakeholders in the length and breadth of the organization by going beyond the boundaries of her job description. This obviously entailed a lot of hard work as this was in addition to excelling in her core job.

Be Prepared to Tell Your Story

You bump into your visiting practice head in the corridor or the elevator and she asks you, 'What's up?' How do you respond to this question?

Having raised this question to thousands of people, the quintessential answer I have invariably heard is:

- All's well

- Going on

- All good

- Nothing much

These responses don't mean much. In fact, they represent a sad loss of an opportunity to promote oneself and make a positive impression on a senior stakeholder.

Share an Achievement

You could leverage this opportunity to your advantage by sharing a quick achievement. For example:

- We are on track to meet our sales target this quarter.

- We are working towards building a healthy sales pipeline.

- We have just tested out an algorithm which will help save substantial time in the order processing system.

Make an Impact

While the above statements send out a positive message, the impact of the message can be enhanced by fortifying it with data. For example:

- We are on track to meet our sales target. We have already met 80 per cent of our quarterly target and we have another month to go.

- We are working towards building a healthy sales pipeline. I am happy to say that just last week we added eight new prospects.

- We have just tested out an algorithm which will help us save 10 seconds per transaction in our order processing system.

Highlight an Activity

The opportunity can be used to highlight an activity that you are preparing for or have engaged in. For example:

- I am excited about our participation in the Globe Tech Engineering Expo at Pune next month. My team is putting up a booth there.

- I am preparing to travel to Australia for the knowledge transfer session for the new accounting process.

- I am back rejuvenated after a trek to the Rajmachi fort.

Build Rapport

Your response can be tailored to build rapport or just establish a connection so that the person remembers you. For example:

- Hi Abdul, I am Thomas Francis. I work for the tax practice in Rupinder's team. I look forward to attending the departmental meeting that you are addressing tomorrow.

- Hello Sara, I had the opportunity to attend your town hall today. Your comments on the economy were particularly insightful.

Dealing with Lack of Response

This could trigger an interaction that may well continue after you have alighted from the elevator. On the other hand, you may not receive an encouraging response in the first place. The person may just nod her head and look elsewhere. But don't allow this to dampen your spirit. Rather than feeling snubbed, assume that the person is preoccupied.

How Much Do I Say?

The answer will be apparent if you pay close attention to the person's body language. For instance, having said, 'What's up?' if the person looks away or gets busy on her mobile phone, it is obvious then that she was not really looking for an answer. But if she smiles and looks up at you, it is a sign that the person is encouraging you to take the dialogue forward.

Be Prepared

- At any point, be prepared with a few headlines related to your key deliverable.
- Know your data like the back of your hand to be able to deliver specific and data-driven statements which have a far greater impact.
- Be audience-centric. Make a quick judgment about what would interest the person.
- Watch the person's body language for pointers around whether you should continue or stop right there.

Speak Up

You need to let go of your diffidence and speak up at forums to be heard and be visible.

Express Your Views

For most part of her career, Bangalore-based Meghna Misra, a senior content marketing strategist at an Indian Fintech company, has been a quiet, diligent worker. She has largely operated with the philosophy that her work will speak for itself and this has manifested in various ways—her reticence at meetings, preference for sharing her ideas over quiet emails and even in the understated approach that she tends to adopt while writing her performance review.

What has held her back from being more open and vocal? 'The fear of being judged,' she said promptly. 'But then I realized that people will judge me anyway. When I don't speak, I am likely to be perceived as not having a view and, therefore, not contributing to a meeting,' she added.

Realizing that it was important for her to promote her work and to be heard in order to get the rewards and recognition commensurate with her work, she made a conscious decision to step out of her comfort zone and be more vocal about her views and work at different forums. And she has sensed immediate, positive results. 'It has not only bolstered my confidence; I also tend to be less defensive and embrace criticism more willingly now. I have also noticed that people are reaching out to me more, involving me in discussions and seeking my opinions.

Ask a Question

'Whom do you recall from the last town hall conference or panel discussion you had attended?' is a question that I have posed to a number of people.

'The speaker and the people who asked questions during the question and answer (Q&A) session,' is the answer that I invariably hear. Evidently, you gain visibility by just raising your hand and asking a question, simply because the majority does not.

What does it take to ask a question? Some preparation in terms of identifying the speakers, reviewing the agenda, thinking on ones feet and, most importantly, overcoming the inner voice that holds you back with doubts like, 'It may not sound smart', 'It does not seem like an intelligent question', 'What will people think?', 'What if...what if...?'

So, the next time you go to these forums, go armed with some questions, determination and the readiness to take the plunge.

Play the Mentor

Your mentees or people you have guided, provided encouragement to and shared knowledge and experiences with, those whose careers you have helped shape are likely to be your greatest advocates. They will promote you by sharing stories about your role in their career development, thereby rendering your brand stronger and more powerful.

A senior vice president at a multinational bank, Chandra Sekhar A. K. N. R.'s narrative below is a case in point.

Chandra acknowledges the roles of several people who have been instrumental in getting him to where he is today. He says,

I met inspiring people along the way, like Managing Director, Sundar Kannan and the then delivery head, Vijayalakshmi at ASM Technologies Ltd, who afforded me immense opportunities for exploring, enhancing and proving my technical prowess.

I would like to acknowledge the mentorship of Sridhar Sunkan and Dan Lejerskar, at EON Reality in Sweden, where I was called upon to work on an interesting project on virtual reality. Lacking cultural intelligence that at time, success would have been highly elusive, had they

not taken me under their wing to help me understand the
nuances of the culture and adapt to it.

I am so grateful to Wayne Mathew, the then delivery lead
at Yokogawa in the UK for allowing me the freedom to
explore and suggest architectural changes and promoting
my contribution to senior management, thus contribut-
ing to my growth, knowledge and confidence.

Take Up a Cause

Nandini Dias, CEO of Loadestar UM, a creative media agency, has the distinction of having managed the media investments of over 175 clients and launching over 400 brands. She has to her credit an array of prestigious awards like the Media Agency of the Year award, Agency CEO of the Year award, besides being recognized as one of the most influential women in the advertising and media industry. To say that she is a big brand is an understatement!

But in the last few years, Dias has been pursuing a cause very close to her heart. 'Why stick to a 9 to 5 schedule that leads to horrendous traffic snarls, choking the roads and train stations? Why not 8 to 4, or may be 11 to 7? How about technology facilitated, work from home approach?' are questions that she has taken to several CEOs and HR heads. With a not inconsiderable investment of time and energy, she has launched a campaign called WorkToLiveToWork, under the aegis of the India chapter of the International Advertising Association, and used her personal influence to advocate staggered or flexible workplace timings.

This pursuance was triggered by a double personal loss. In November 2016, Dias's brother, Dhananjay Bansod, had lost his life at Dadar station in Mumbai. Caught in a whirl-pool of people trying to get into a train, he lost his balance and his head hit the railing of the foot bridge on that fateful day. About 10 months later, Dias's colleague lost her life in the stampede that had played out at Elphinstone station at Mumbai. This double loss got Dias thinking and reimagining a corporate workday.

With a passionate and relentless pursuit of this cause, Dias incorporated the dimension of a crusader to her persona; thus adding richness, diversity and visibility to her brand.

Apprise Your Stakeholders

Arvind Charanyan V., a senior leader at a fashion and lifestyle e-commerce portal says,

I think leveraging the right forums to promote your work to your stakeholders is critical, not from the perspective of being in the limelight, but for looping them in to gain alignment. I regularly hold 'road shows' inviting our internal stakeholders, as well as external partners, and have the team apprise them of progress and noteworthy wins, in addition to the issues they may be grappling with.

According to Charanyan, it is a good opportunity to solicit feedback and understand expectations to be able to make any mid-course corrections, if required. These engagements go a long way in minimizing surprises by getting all the stakeholders on the same page, besides motivating and energizing the team as it gets to communicate with the stakeholders directly and hear first-hand from them.

Engage on Internal Organizational Platforms

Share Your Stories

Vrinda Mariwala, a manager in the IT function transformation team in a global consulting firm, had the opportunity to work on a process automation project, using robotic process automation, a new, cutting-edge technology in this space, for a large company located in Kazakhstan. She says,

It took me three connecting flights and a six-hour road journey to get to the project site which was located in the interiors of the country. The project turned out to be extremely enriching, not only from the technical perspective, but also in terms of learning how to overcome cultural barriers and work effectively in a non-English speaking country.

Upon her return to India, Mariwala took time to reflect on the project and drafted her experience, along with her take-aways, sanitized it and posted it as a use case on the firm's intranet. Her post evoked a lot of interest in the global organizational community, with people, including senior partners, reaching out to her with questions and drawing her into keen discussions on the project. This gave her immense visibility and helped her forge connections with people in the global community, which held her in good stead later whenever she needed some information or expert advice. She says,

We have several internal collaboration platforms—both India specific and global—where you are invited to showcase your white papers and stories pertaining to interesting projects and client engagements. I have found value in engaging on these platforms as it affords both visibility and opportunities to connect with colleagues around the world, who you may not otherwise get a chance to interact with.

Engage on Discussion Forums

Shruti Das, a senior technology manager at a global bank, spoke about the different forums provided by the bank to enable people to showcase their expertise. 'I was a part of the committee that launched a forum called SME (Subject Matter Expert), where domain and technology experts could post technical articles and white papers, obtain opportunities to speak on technology trends, and even run training programs to help others come up to speed with new technologies. The forum had roped in expert facilitators, to groom people who had the technical expertise, but lacked facilitation skills.

By engaging on the forum, people not only got recognition for their technical expertise, they also got opportunities to build their networks by engaging with people in other teams and verticals, with whom they may never have had an occasion to engage otherwise,' said Das.

A manager at an investment bank spoke about the discussion groups within the technology practice that had been formed for different technologies such as Python, .Net, artificial intelligence and machine language. People in these groups engaged in discussions, conducted knowledge-sharing sessions, posted interesting pieces of code and white papers in that space, organized quizzes and responded to questions posted by people. This enabled them to engage with a wider community, showcase their technical proficiency, build their networks and gain visibility.

Participate in CSR Activities

Nikhil D'souza, a manager working for an FMCG company, who has distinguished himself in the area of CSR space, spoke with me about his engagement in this space.

'Our company has a robust CSR forum here in Mumbai, where we have tied up with a few schools and vocational colleges that cater to children and women with economically challenged backgrounds. The vocational colleges provide courses in computer applications, tailoring, nursing and accounting to help women launch their professional careers. Our team was instrumental in devising a curriculum encompassing English-speaking, interviewing skills and confidence building to prepare them for job interviews. The results have been very encouraging with women getting placed as administrative assistants, librarians and accountants in different schools and companies.'

'Additionally, I also got involved in rallying task forces comprising volunteers from the company to engage in periodic beach clean-up activities in collaboration with an NGO,' said Nikhil.

'What is in it for him as this must mean a considerable investment of time and energy?'

'Besides being an immensely valuable opportunity to pursue my passion for community service, participation in these activities has helped me hone my confidence, build my network and gain visibility with people across levels in different parts of the organization. I have had a chance to interact with so many people with whom I would never have crossed paths otherwise. Recently, I was also recognized for my participation with the prestigious CSR award instituted by the company,' he said with a smile.

Engage in Extracurricular Activities

Shyamala Chetri, a manager in the technology team of a global bank, gained immense visibility through her participation in organizational events.

'My manager was organizing a town hall for our visiting practice head and was looking for someone who could host the event. I was tempted to put up my hand, but my self-doubts held me back as I had never hosted such an event before. But I saw an opportunity in the challenge to try my hand at doing something different. So, stepping out of my comfort zone, I took the plunge. The town hall went well and turned out to be immensely successful and a great booster for my newly found confidence. And suddenly, I found myself highly visible within the group!

Riding on the wave of this success, my next opportunity came when I was asked to host the Technology Talent Show with an anticipated audience of about 500. I invested time watching a number of shows on YouTube, picking up catchy lines and adapting them to our event. Working very hard, I rehearsed several times over. The event was a grand success and I was applauded by the senior leaders who were present at the show. One of my colleagues even commented, "Shyamala, in my four years with this group, I haven't gained as much visibility as you have in four months!" People began to see me as creative, outgoing and always up for a challenge.

I had become the de facto employee engagement manager for our team. During the COVID-19 lockout, therefore, when our entire team was working from home, my manager entrusted me with engaging the group with some innovative, daily touch points. Responding to the challenge once again, I organized daily, 15-minute, virtual coffee sessions for our 50-people strong team around themes like, "your fitness mantra," "engaging your kids during lockdown" and "your biggest learning from the lockdown." It gave people an opportunity to share experiences, hear from each other and stay connected. This was another engagement which gave me a lot of visibility,' says Chetri.

Participate in Social Clubs

Organizations offer forums to enable people to pursue their personal interests and engage in leisure activities. For instance, at a global consulting company, the foodies' club members get together and explore different eating places and then post their experiences and recommendations on the intranet. Similarly, there's the bikers' club, the hikers' club and the runners' club. The photographer's club holds photo exhibition and photography contests on different themes periodically, thus presenting people a platform to display their talent. In fact, people in this club have become the de facto photographers for important company events, giving them a chance to showcase their talent to a wider audience, gain visibility, build their networks and add a side hustle to their personal brand.

Other Platforms

A participant at one of my programs spoke about a forum called the International Association Network offered by his company. People opting for this forum are randomly paired with a person from a different domain, service line and location. 'I had been paired with someone from our Australia office, providing me a chance to exchange ideas with a person in another part of the organization, learn about a different domain and understand the nuances of a different culture. This relationship became a stepping stone for connecting with another team in Australia when I had to reach out to them in the context of a project I was working on,' he said.

Engage on the Social Media

The social media is a powerful platform to build your brand and gain visibility by demonstrating your expertise and the value that you represent.

'Engaging on the social media has been a big learning for me. You may be good at something but for people to find value in it, they need to first know of your existence. Social media can play an important role in building brand visibility,' says Kamat.

This has been discussed in greater details in the next chapter.

- Make a list of your wins and achievements during the last three months. Think of project completions, sales deals, process improvement initiatives, cost alleviation measures, difficult client conversations and the like. Then think through the following.

  o Who needs to know about these wins? Think of stakeholders in your local office, regional office, head office and clients.

  o Identify ways of communicating your achievements. For example,

    ▪ Write your story on the company's internal website,

    ▪ Add the story to one of your presentations to these stakeholders,

    ▪ Communicate the achievement through an email and

    ▪ Think of other channels.

- Introspect on the following points with respect to the last important meeting that you had attended.

  o Were you well prepared?

  o Did you contribute to the discussion?

  o Did you leverage this meeting to make an impact?

- Prepare your story.

- o Write down some points about your possible response to the question, 'What's up?' from a stakeholder. Think of your recent achievements and headlines related to your key deliverables.

- List down the forums or internal platforms offered by your company that you could leverage to showcase your achievements, display your talents, meet people and gain visibility.

- A well thought-out strategy for communicating your achievements, strengths and talents to your stakeholders is imperative for gaining recognition and promoting your brand.

- The idea of self-promotion may feel uncomfortable. Therefore, reframe it in your mind and think of it as a mutually beneficial communication that not only helps you gain recognition and visibility, but also equips your stakeholders with data points to enable them to make better and sounder decisions.

- Ways to promote yourself without appearing to toot your horn:

  - o Communicate your achievements through anecdotes. Spin a story around how you overcame a challenge, and evoke the interest of the audience by lacing it with characters, suspense and drama, and above all, ensure that it is relevant for your audience and they find value in it.

  - o Give your ideas a chance to be recognized and taken forward by presenting them to the right audience at the right forum.

o Gain recognition by imparting greater visibility to ideas borrowed from others by presenting them to a wider audience.

o Promote yourself by going beyond your job description. Put your hand up for cross-functional projects, for instance, as this would not only provide you an opportunity to display your talent and expertise to a broader audience, but also help build your network by connecting with people in another part of the organization.

o 'How are things going?' is a frequently encountered question. Leverage this opportunity to build rapport or to promote yourself by sharing some quick data points about your achievements and key deliverables, instead of frittering it away by saying something insipid like 'All good.' Be audience-centric and use your discretion to figure out what and how much you will say to whom.

o Make an impact by speaking up at meetings, expressing your views and contributing to discussions.

o Play the mentor and help shape someone's career. The person is likely to promote you by sharing stories about your mentorship.

o Take up a cause. This will not only give you purpose beyond your job role but also help strengthen your brand by adding another dimension.

o Be proactive in seeking meetings to brief your stakeholders and leverage the forum to promote yourself by sharing progress, achievements as well as challenges.

o Engage on internal organizational platforms to showcase your talent, expertise and project wins. Participate in CSR activities, social clubs, discussion forums and training platforms.

References

1. Gartner [Internet]. Gartner says CMOs remain confident amid leveled off budgets and uncertain times. 8 Nov 2018. Available from: https://www.gartner.com/en/newsroom/press-releases/2018-10-08-gartner-says-cmos-remain-confident-amid-leveled-off-budgets-and-uncertain-times
2. Friedman TL. It's a flat world, after all. The New York Times Magazine [Internet]. 3 April 2005. Available from: https://www.nytimes.com/2005/04/03/magazine/its-a-flat-world-after-all.html

Chapter 10

The Power of Social Media
Amplify Your Reach

How do you leverage the social platform effectively? How do you find the sweet spot or the vantage point that affords a good view and enables you to portray your skills and expertise, talents and strengths and products and services to your target audience in an effectual manner?

Rudyard Kipling provides some pertinent clues to these questions in the below couplet from the story 'The Elephant's Child', published as a part of *Just so Stories*, a collection of short stories written for children in 1902.[1]

> 'I keep six honest serving-men
> (They taught me all I knew);
> Their names are What and Why and When
> And How and Where and Who.'

Today, social media is deemed to be the foremost and one of the most important platforms for connecting, interacting, engaging, presenting and communicating. It's a valuable forum to build and promote your brand, by depicting who you are, what you stand for and the skills and expertise that you bring to the table. It amplifies your capacity to reach out to an audience far beyond your primary network, but it is a crowded place, with people jostling for room, vying for attention and being wooed by a gamut of competing social media channels.

The road map for engaging on the social media lies in finding answers to the 'what, why, when, how, where and who' of your proposed engagement.

Why?

What is your purpose? Why do you want to be there? What are you hoping to achieve? Nailing this down is the crucial first step for diving successfully into this large, deep sea called the social media.

Who are you?

Next, design and present a compelling profile outlining your expertise, skills and experience tailored to your purpose.

Who's your audience?

Who should know about you, your skills and your expertise? Who do you want to present yourself to? So, identify your target audience.

How?

A critical next step is to figure out your messaging strategy. How will you communicate your expertise, value, skills and intellectual capability to your target audience in a manner that is constructive and helpful, and does not sound self-aggrandizing?

Where?

There's a spectrum of social media channels out there calling loudly for attention. Which of these will you get on to? Since certain channels lend themselves naturally to specific types of communication and presentation, your choice of channel or channels will largely be guided by your purpose.

When?

How often should you engage? It is imperative to find the right balance as social media engagement entails an investment of time and effort. Moreover, you run the risk of evoking audience fatigue by engaging once too often and being obliterated from their minds by engaging erratically or infrequently.

Your Engagement Strategy

It is important to draw up a carefully curated engagement strategy that addresses your purpose and helps portray your knowledge, skills and value in the most impactful and compelling manner that would help you develop and strengthen the brand that you are seeking to build.

Define Your Purpose

There could be multifarious reasons for you to want to get on to the social media bandwagon, such as:

- Being recognized as an expert or a thought leader in your domain, thereby building your brand

- Discovering new job opportunities

- Obtaining referrals to grow your business

- Expressing your thoughts and ideas

- Augmenting your knowledge

Your engagement strategy is the outcome of your purpose, which itself can change over time and evolve as you walk a few exploratory steps to test waters, as demonstrated in the stories below.

Chandoo

Chandoo.org, with over 50,000 members and 1.6 million visits every month, offers tips, tutorials, online training programs and project and portfolio management templates in Excel, Visual Basic for Applications and Power Pivot. An 11-time recipient of the prestigious Microsoft Most Valuable Professional award, Chandoo's rendezvous with the social media started in 2004 as a blogger while at B-school. His blog was a medley of personal experiences, thoughts, observations and perspectives aimed at sharing an insider perspective about life at B-school with family and friends. 'Six months into blogging, I decided to register my website. Since my full name, Purna Chandra Rao Duggirala, is quite a mouthful, I decided to use my nickname for the website,' says Chandoo. Chadoo.org was thus born.

After joining TCS as a business analyst, Chandoo kept his website going with his personal stories, experiences and other trivia. Chandoo's camaraderie with Excel started in 2007, when he started using it extensively in his work. His mind would constantly play the acrobat, the juggler and the tightrope walker in the realm of Excel, understanding, exploring and teasing out the nuances and their application. Gradually, he started sharing his Excel-related insights and discoveries on his website, giving it a more serious, technical and Excel-centric flavour.

Subsequently, the traffic on the website started growing as more and more people read, engaged and asked questions. 'Getting a sense that people were finding value in my posts, I was driven to post more technical content, and the harder I worked the more traction I got,' says Chandoo. Soon, he launched an online training program in Excel and subsequently introduced ready templates for managing projects and portfolios, all of which had ready takers. This success enabled Chandoo to muster the strength and confidence to opt out of a thriving career with TCS and focus full time on Chandoo.org. What started as a personal, casual website is the core of a multimillion-dollar enterprise today. Chandoo is also active on LinkedIn and has a thriving YouTube channel. He says,

When I started blogging I had no thought or intention about starting a business or building my brand. I was just penning down my thoughts and ideas for what was largely a personal network. In hindsight, this casual rendezvous with blogging not only gave me a platform for channelizing my thoughts, it also helped me hone my writing skills and gain visibility within my personal and professional community. Brand building, thus, happened as a happy corollary.

Abhijit Bhaduri

Abhijit Bhaduri is a talent management practitioner, an author of two books *The Digital Tsunami* and *Don't Hire the Best—How to Hire for Culture Fit*, a columnist for several newspapers and the former chief learning officer of Wipro. He had featured on LinkedIn Top Voices—the 15 must-know writers in India in 2016, was identified as one of Society for Human Resource Management's top 50 HR influencers on the social media in 2018 and has 850,000 followers on LinkedIn and Twitter.

'My primary objective in engaging on the social media was to learn. Everything else has happened as a by-product,' says Bhaduri. His tryst with the social media started as a blogger way back in 2005, soon after which he set up his own website, before starting to dabble with Twitter. He says,

I consider Twitter as one of the most powerful tools for informal, unstructured learning, as there are no boundaries, and you are free to follow anybody you wish. As an enthusiastic beginner I started by following some 90 people. That was a mistake. Realizing that, I altered

my approach and became more selective, identifying just 25 people I wanted to follow.

Vijayraj Kamat

Vijayraj Kamat's day job revolved around interplaying data analytics and block chain technology for designing innovative IT solutions and managing multiple stakeholders at large, global businesses during his tenure with Deloitte. But his core interest lay in psychology and spirituality. He discovered *Quora*, an online question and answer (Q&A) forum and a meeting place for the world's best minds to engage in discussions on almost everything under the sun, in 2014. 'In Quora, I found an avenue for expressing my thoughts and sharing my ideas. I would park any question that I found inspirational and respond to it late into the night after completing my day job,' says Kamat.

In less than 2 years, he penned down more than a thousand articles, demystifying complex and nebulous issues like ways to attain success and happiness, deal with different life challenges and prioritize and manage life in general. From general questions like 'Is India forgetting its culture?' to life-related question like 'What is our purpose on this earth?' he answered them all. The response from his readers acknowledging the depth and usefulness of his answers was enough to keep him going.

Then magic happened one day when his answer to the question 'How can I explain to a ten-year-old as to why a US dollar costs 60 INR?' went viral with over 800,000 views and 36,000 upvotes, catapulting his following from about 100 to 4,000. And in 2017–2018, at 4,500+ followers, he became a Quora Top Writer, cementing his brand on the forum.

Chetna Vasishth

After a successful run as a banker, a faculty at IIM Bangalore and a training and development consultant, Chetna Vasishth today runs

ChetChat, one of India's top online chat shows in the career and education space. Since its launch in 2015, the show has featured over 200 videos with more than 5 million views and has over 1 million subscribers.

Vasishth uses videos to engage with the youth on a variety of topics like how to stay motivated, build confidence, hone English-speaking skills, inculcate the habits of highly successful students, prepare an effective timetable to study for an exam and read and remember a text book, amongst others.

Choose Your Channel

There are umpteen platforms on the social media that you can get on to. But four channels stand out from a professional engagement standpoint. These have been discussed further.

LinkedIn

LinkedIn is primarily a professional social media site, considered as a de facto point of reference for any professional today. In fact, it is odd for a professional to not have presence on LinkedIn. The channel lends itself well for enabling you to establish your brand by demonstrating your skills, knowledge and thought leadership. You can engage, connect and communicate with your professional ecosystem comprising colleagues, professional associates, recruiters and current and potential business partners. Similarly, companies can leverage LinkedIn to build their brand and establish their industry leadership by presenting their products, services, activities that are innovative and noteworthy, industry trends and their valued proposition to their employees and business partners.

LinkedIn offers a formal, workplace-like environment where communication primarily centres around professional stories and insights, intellectual and developmental pursuits, domain-related discussions, achievements, certifications, awards and recognition. You can communicate freely only with those you are connected with, unlike Twitter where you are at liberty to follow anyone. A connection is solicited through a formal invite, thus rendering the connections bilateral and mutual.

Twitter

Twitter as a platform is a more conversational, where you can not only engage in business or professional conversations but also in discussions on topics as diverse as current affairs, sports, entertainment, politics and economy. Communication tends to be in real time, with local and global events posted and discussed almost instantaneously. You can demonstrate your domain prowess by sharing domain-related trends and developments along with your comments, views and perspectives. You can also reveal your personal side by sharing your activities, thoughts and achievements in your personal-interest areas. By following the right people, you can keep yourself abreast of trends, events and other updates in your domain or spheres of interest.

You are free to follow anyone on Twitter, with a restriction of 280 characters for a tweet.

Instagram

Taking a page from Street Railway Advertising's National Advertising Manager, Fred R. Bernard's famous 1921 quote, 'One look is worth a thousand words', Instagram offers a visually oriented platform that can help you bring your personal, product and corporate stories to life by facilitating their presentation through photos and videos. The platform has gained popularity not only in visually driven domains like fashion, travel and beauty but also in other domains where individuals as well as companies leverage it progressively more for sharing their policies, goals, achievements and value proposition. Companies even run thematic engagement programs inviting employees to display their talents and expertise on Instagram.

YouTube

YouTube is a video-sharing platform that allows you to communicate your stories and demonstrate your skills, knowledge and domain expertise through videos. The videos can be uploaded on your YouTube channel, which people can either subscribe to, or just browse through, casually. Your channel could start generating revenue if it elicits significant audience interest and garners substantial subscriptions to attract potential advertisers.

Thus, based on your intent, purpose and comfort, you may choose to engage on a single or a variety of channels on the social media. Consider the following examples:

- Alok Jha, an HR veteran and an alumnus of global organizations such as Datamatics Global Services, LafargeHolcim Ltd, Poonawalla Group, Siemens Atos and Al Faisal Holding, demonstrates his prowess and thought leadership through his weekly video posts on wide-ranging themes in the realm of HR and workplace excellence on LinkedIn.

- Vasishht of ChetChat has chosen to communicate her ideas and engage with her audience, comprising students on the anvil of launching their careers, through videos. Her preferred social media platform is YouTube.

- Kamat's tryst with the social media started with LinkedIn and Quora. As an IT professional, he connected on LinkedIn, but since his interest also lay in communicating with people on deeper and nebulous topics such as attainment of success, happiness and excellence, he chose Quora additionally. But once he took the plunge to transition from an IT career into a full-time career in the area of people and organizational development, he sought to rebrand himself from a 'techy' to an 'organizational development consultant' brand, actively leveraging LinkedIn for doing so.

- Chandoo uses both the written word and videos for posting his content and engaging with his audience. Therefore, while his website Chandoo.org is the primary platform for communication, he has a powerful LinkedIn presence and a thriving YouTube channel where he frequently posts videos unravelling the nuances of Excel for his audience.

- While Twitter continues to be Bhaduri's preferred platform on the social media, he also has a strong presence on LinkedIn and Instagram. A talented artist and a cartoonist, Bhaduri has over 500 posts and sketchnotes (Mike Rohde, author of the bestselling book, *The Sketchnote Handbook*, explains sketchnotes as 'rich visual notes created from a mix of handwriting, drawings, hand-drawn typography, shapes, and visual elements like arrows, boxes, and lines') on the social media on varied topics like leadership, workplace and personal effectiveness and current affairs.

Post a Powerful Profile

Your rendezvous with any social media platform starts with an introduction. Post a profile that differentiates you, helps build your credibility and does justice to who you are. The following discussion pertains to a profile on LinkedIn since it is considered the de facto point of reference for most people in the corporate world, but the same principles hold for designing profiles for any platform.

Keep It Current

It is not uncommon to find professionals represented by profiles that are obsolete and antiquated. Their typical response to the question, 'When was the last time you had updated your profile?' is 'When I had last set out job hunting.'

This view is rather myopic and certainly not a strategy for success. You don't update your profile when seeking new job opportunities. Rather you build your profile over time to help potential recruiters support you in finding the right opportunities. Besides, recruitment is not the only reason for keeping your profile current and vibrant. Remember that your profile serves as a ready reckoner for your ecosystem which is constantly accessing it in a host of different contexts. What message would an outdated profile send out? It would paint a person not particularly concerned about how they are perceived and, therefore, lacking a sharp focus on career management.

Photo: The First Visual

The first element on your profile that hits the eye and draws instant attention is your profile photo. Ensure that the photo shows you as the person you are today, rather than what you may have looked like 20 years ago. People should be able to recognize you from the photo.

* *Post a photo*

  Experts say that simply having a photo can obtain 21 times more profile views and 9 times more connection requests. I am surprised at the number of people who simply don't have one on their profile!

- *First impression*

Post a good quality headshot photo that portrays you as personable and professional because first impressions matter!

Vivian Zayas, an associate professor in psychology at Cornell University, did an interesting study which established that first impressions gathered from a person's photo tend to stick on even after a personal interaction with the person at a later point. In the study, 55 participants were shown two pictures each of four women, with the women smiling in the first picture and donning a neutral expression in the second. See Figure 10.1. Subsequently, the participants were asked to evaluate them on parameters such as likeability and personality traits like extroversion, emotional stability and conscientiousness. One-to-six months later, the participants were asked to evaluate the women on the same parameters again, after they had had a personal interaction with them. It was found that their impressions had remained unchanged (see Figure 10.1).[2]

Figure 10.1. Picture Used in Vivian Zayas's Study

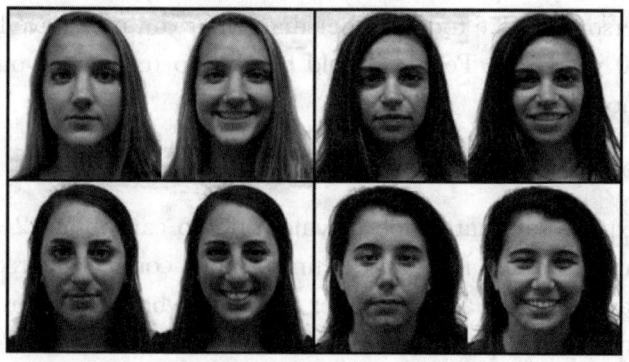

Source: Cornell Chronicle. https://news.cornell.edu/stories/2016/11/even-after-having-read-book-one-still-judges-it-its-cover

- *Likeability*

  What expression should you wear in the photo? There is evidence to show that compared with any other expression, a smiling face is perceived as more friendly and personable.

  Photofeeler, a portal that provides people anonymous feedback on their photos, conducted a study wherein they captured 60,000 ratings from people on 800 profile photos based on their perception of the person on three parameters— competence, likeability and influence. The study found that photos of people with a smile got a higher rating and those smiling with teeth visible, a much higher rating on all the three parameters!

- *Professionalism*

  While your attire should be aligned with the established norms of your industry, the same study revealed that, irrespective of industry, a person who was formally attired was perceived as not only more competent but also more influential.

- *Prominence of face*

  It is recommended that all the background noise be clipped out so that your face stands out as the most prominent element in the photo, taking up 60 per cent of the photo slot.

Background Picture: The Second Visual

LinkedIn allows you to post a background visual just behind the photo. This can be leveraged to highlight an achievement, a talent, a value that you endorse or a product or service you are associated with. LinkedIn recommends using a .Png, .Jpj or a .Gif image with a 1,400x425 resolution for best effect.

The two visuals—the photo and the background picture—should work in tandem in terms of content, colour and presentation to

Figure 10.2. Photo with Background Picture

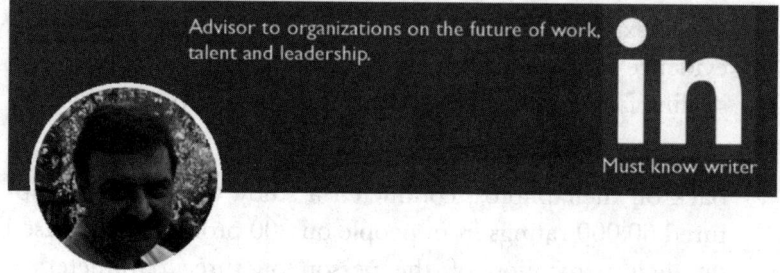

reinforce your message. Rather than competing for attention, the two need to be in perfect sync. The photo, in fact, should command a little more attention, with the background picture playing a supportive role.

- In Figure 10.2, Abhijit Bhaduri's photo and background picture stand in perfect harmony. While the photo is prominent, the simple, clean and uncluttered background visual very subtly draws attention to two key messages.

  - Recognition as a writer

    Bhaduri had featured on LinkedIn Top Voices: The 15 must-know writers in India in 2016.

  - Services offered

    Bhaduri provides advisory services to organizations on the future of work, talent and leadership.

- In Figure 10.3, the wing of a plane as the background picture points to Harsha Jhunjhunwala's global experience, having worked for clients in 12 different geographies. Note that the background picture makes the point without distracting attention from the photo.

Figure 10.3. Photo with Background Picture

The Headline

Headline is the caption that appears on the top of your profile page just below the name. It is important to design this judiciously, within the 120 character limit, to provide the reader a snapshot of your profession, role, key skills and other engagements such as writing, speaking, consulting and training, as this is displayed, along with your name and photo, in the search results of both LinkedIn and Google. Incorporating your domain and industry-related keywords in your headline will facilitate search. Consider the examples below.

- **Example 1**
  - **Ashutosh Rane**
    Associate Director at *Name of the company*

  - **Sneha Duggal**
    Director at *Name of the company*

    The headlines above are scanty, scarcely telling the reader anything beyond the person's designation and company.

- **Example 2**
  - **Ashutosh Rane**

> Associate Director | Name of the company | Integrated SAP solutions specialist | Global clients

- **Sneha Duggal**

  Director | Name of company | Financial Reporting, Auditing and Taxation specialist | large public and private companies

  By offering the reader additional data points, these headlines are more informative.

- **Example 3**

  - **Rahul Das**

    BTech, MTech, MBA, PMP, PMI-ACP, PSM, DBF, ITIL, ISTQB, CFA, Project Manager, Consultant, Name of company

    Remember, it is not just what you say but also how you say that determines impact.

    i. Too much information overwhelms the reader; so instead of going overboard, use your discretion to eliminate repetitious data points that don't add value. For instance, in this headline, the words 'BTech' and 'Consultant' can be removed without loss of substance.

    ii. It is important to space out the content to enhance readability. See example below.

  - **Rahul Das**

    Project Manager | *Name of company* | MTech | PMP | PMI–ACP | PSM | DBF | ITIL | ISTQB | CFA

- **Example 4**

  - **Seema Malhotra**

    15+ Years' Experience | Result Driven | Machine Learning | Data Science | Predictive Analytics

Starting with the number of years of experience sounds a bit odd. Start with role, company and then move to skills, specialization and other talents. 'Result driven' can be included elsewhere in the profile.

- **Seema Malhotra**

  Data Scientist | Name of the company

  Machine learning | Predictive analysis | 15+ Years' Experience

- **Example 5**

  - **Purna Duggirala**

    Chandoo.org ▪ Microsoft MVP ▪ Excel, VBA & Power BI Trainer ▪ Blogger ▪ Entrepreneur ▪ YouTuber

    This presents a simple, clean and informative headline.

The Summary

The summary is an important element of your profile that provides the reader a run through of your professional journey in 2,000 characters. It is a clean slate that can be painted any way you wish. In effect, it should be designed to answer the 'tell me something about yourself' question. This is your chance to highlight your experience, skills and accolades and reveal your passion, talents and interesting personality traits to provide the reader a well-rounded view of who you are. There are no restrictive boundaries in terms of dates and organizations that need to be adhered to, but these can be stated to give your narrative a context. Given below are some good practices for drafting an impactful summary.

- *Post a summary*

  In the first place, do post a summary. It is surprising to see the number of people who skip this important element in their profiles. A wasted opportunity indeed!

- *Write it as you would say it*

  Writing the summary in first person sounds more real and helps you connect with the reader better.

- *Give it some thought*

  I came across one-liner summaries, like the one below, on a vast number of profiles on LinkedIn. The summary warrants some serious thought and deserves to be articulated as more than just a headline.

  A chartered accountant specializing in the field of Indirect taxes.

- *Add a specialties section*

  A neat way to bundle in all your technical and domain skills in a single or a couple of rows is to use the specialities section at the end of the summary. This also makes it easy for the audience to see all your skills at one glance. See the example below.

  Marketing specialties

  Marketing innovation | Digital marketing | Digital transformation | Market intelligence | Strategic partnerships | Customer insights

- *Say it with a story*

  Stories get people interested and infuse life into your narrative. Consider the examples below.

Example 1

A technophile, I am powered by continuous learning and driven by values.

My 25-year long journey in IT entailed successful project delivery in the areas of:

- Virtual Reality (DirectX, D3D, C++)

- Industrial Automation (OPC, C++)

- Retail Banking—Cards, Channels (Cloud computing, Data)

I have had several opportunities during the course of my career to prove my entrepreneurial leadership by way of:

- Setting up offshore teams

- Managing platform budgets in the north of $10 million/annum

- Leveraging the Core Competency Model for drawing up the offshore workforce strategy

- Designing and implementing an Engineering Score Card capturing four dimensions—Better–Faster–Cheaper–Engaged

My passion, as a technocrat, lies in leveraging the 'ABCDE' of technology—Augmented Reality, Blockchain, Cloud Computing, Data and Edutainment—to help organizations in their digital transformation journey.

I strongly believe in building trust through openness, honesty and participative feedback. I invest time and energy coaching and grooming people and engaging with the student community at colleges sharing my knowledge, explaining the principles of collaborative lateral thinking and the importance of learning from nature around us.

My family gives me an extra edge and I consider it as the soul of my success.

This summary gives a robust view of the person as it highlights:

1. **Technologies** the person's conversant with

2. **Experience** in setting up teams, managing budgets, drawing up workforce strategies and designing and implementing a project performance score card

3. **Passion** for learning—the term 'technophile' indicates that strongly

4. **Interest** in developing people

5. **Value** which places family at the centre of success

Example 2

I let go of a thriving technology career to pursue my passion for helping organizations develop better leaders and teams.

My technology career entailed delivering cross-sectoral, multi-technology projects to global clients which afforded me a good insight into business challenges. It helped me realize that systems and processes are mere business enablers, and the key to success really lies in the seamless alignment of people with business goals.

Recognizing that my interest lay in the 'people' side of business, I started working towards honing my people development skills and took the plunge to embark on a full-time career in people and organizational development in 2014. The journey since has been extremely enriching, exciting and challenging, as I have been constantly called upon to step right out of my comfort zone to provide solutions in a variety of different contexts.

I am particularly proud of my work in the areas of:

• Gender and inter-generational diversity

• Personal branding and executive presence

Given below is the repertoire of services that I provide:

• 1:1 Coaching

  Helping people find their paths for transcending personal and professional roadblocks that impede success.

• Training

  o Leadership

- Managing 360—Self, peers, senior stakeholders, teams and customer
- Enabling teams in inculcating the value of collaboration for producing better business results
  - Professional skills
    - Personal brand
    - Managing difficult conversations
    - Networking
    - Influencing
    - Presenting with impact
  - Diversity
    - Gender
    - Inter-generational

I have a green thumb, am a fitness freak and enjoy jazz and blues music.

Specialities

Published articled in leading newspapers | TEDx speaker | Certified on DISC, Hogan | Visiting faculty at business schools

This is an example of a well-rounded summary that is likely to hold the reader's interest for the following reasons:

1. Narrates a story highlighting the drivers for a career transition
2. States core strengths and services provided
3. Highlights other important engagements like writing, speaking, teaching and certifications
4. Provides a deeper insight about the person by stating interests outside work
5. Uses industry-related keywords that facilitate search

- *Work experience*

  Capture your work history, outlining your career progression with details of each job in terms of roles, responsibilities and accomplishments. Use your discretion to figure out the extent of details to present. Elaborate on the ones that help paint your current profile and are more significant and relevant from your current brand perspective, skipping details of those that go way back in time or not so relevant in the current context.

  Harsha Jhunjhunwala has supplemented the headline, summary and work experience with a work experience summary which provides the reader a pictorial snapshot of her professional profile.

- *Other tips*

  o Use rich media

    Complementing your narrative with relevant videos, audios, presentations and articles not only strengthens

Figure 10.4. Experience Summary

In search of the next frontier of emerging technologies

Harsha Jhunjhunwala
PwC | IIM | DA-IICT

Technology strategist

8+ years
Mumbai, India

- IT, digital and emerging technology strategy
- Enterprise architecture
- Business process automation
- Transformation management
- Post-acquisition integration
- Digital procurement and governance
- Technology cost management

- TOGAF 9.2
- PMP
- PRINCE2 Practitioner
- COBIT5 Foundation
- ITIL v3 Foundation

- Pharmaceuticals
- Manufacturing
- Logistics
- Real-estate
- Technology & ITeS

- Jamaica
- Kazakhstan
- Philippines
- UAE
- Singapore

- Design thinking
- Mind mapping
- Story telling

your message but also captures the audience's interest by bringing your story to life.

o Include the right keywords

Think through your domain or industry-related keywords relevant to your profile and use these extensively in your Headline, Summary and Experience to ensure that you show up higher on LinkedIn and Google search results.

o Keep it brief

Leverage the principles of brevity and simplicity as repetitive and unnecessary words annoy readers, slow them down and distract them from the key message. Be ruthless in eliminating unnecessary words without compromising on the essence of the message. Use bullets for a more crisp presentation wherever appropriate.

o Proofread

Spelling and grammatical errors are eyesores that distract the reader, mitigate the effectiveness of your narrative and point to sloppiness and a lack of attention to detail. It is worthwhile, therefore, to invest time proofreading your write-up.

o Customize your LinkedIn URL

A customized URL that includes your name (www. linkedin.com/in/yourname) looks neater and more professional when you include it in your email signature, business card and other social media channels.

Build Your Network

You have identified the appropriate channels, posted a powerful profile and are now ready to engage. But whom will you engage with? Who's your target audience?

It is important to start building your network by connecting with people who you think you should be engaging with based on your domain, areas of expertise and your goals. Once connected, you can see the person's complete profile, can message directly and have access to their network.

Reach Out

- A good starting point would be to reach out to people who are known to you—people in your ecosystem like your current and former colleagues, industry associates, clients, suppliers and the like.

- Follow the practice of connecting with people you meet at conferences, industry event and in other contexts. Reach out to those who resonate within 24 hours of the meeting while they still remember you.

- Review the 'people you may know' list that the LinkedIn algorithm furnishes from time to time based on commonalities identified from your academic and professional career and take the initiative to connect with them at your discretion.

Sending a personalized request as opposed to LinkedIn's default 'I'd like to join your LinkedIn network' is more fruitful as it is more encouraging for people to respond positively to your invite. For instance, one of my program participants categorically stated, 'If I get a request with a personal note, I always consider accepting it even if I don't know the person.'

It is, thus, helpful to send a request through a personal note stating the context. Consider the examples below:

- I hope you remember our meeting at the ABC conference yesterday. It would be good to connect on LinkedIn.

- I have been reading your very insightful posts on blockchain technology. This is an area of particular interest to me and

I am currently trying to learn more about this technology. I hope you will accept my invite for connecting on LinkedIn.

- I thought it will be good to connect as we are in the same profession.

- I look forward to connecting with you since we are both members of the ABC group on LinkedIn.

But don't be too ruffled if people don't accept your invite. Some are busy and some are not very active on the social media and there's a chance that the person has not even seen your invite. Be prepared to wait, and then move on without giving it another thought. Don't forget to send a thank you note when a person accepts your invite.

Respond to Requests

As you start engaging, you will receive connection requests from others. How do you respond to these requests?

People you know

This is easy. You simply go ahead and accept the request.

People you don't know

This can be tricky! What criteria will you use to respond to such requests? I posed this question to a few people and obtained the below responses.

- o I look for commonalities—employer, college, school, group, activities, domain and common connections. If I find even a remotely common touch point, I accept.

- o I accept requests from people in the corporate world, consultants, coaches and students as they are the future leaders.

o   If I get a request with a personal note, I will certainly consider it even if I don't know the person. I ignore the others.

o   I accept requests from individuals and ignore the ones from company profiles. What is the cost of accepting a connect that may not be relevant? I will probably receive some annoying communication around selling a product or service that doesn't interest me. In such a case I can exercise the option of disconnecting. I don't think it is worth thinking too much since the cost in terms of the time spent in evaluation far outweighs the benefit of eliminating an irrelevant connect.

o   I prefer to exercise caution and be more selective since the composition of my network reflects on my brand.

So, people have different views and approaches based on their context, mindset and personality.

I tend to be more open and mostly use my gut while responding to requests, turning down only those that are outrageously random. For instance, why would a trader from Timbuktoo want to connect with me?

I follow the practice of accepting a request with a thank you note such as, 'Hi, thanks for reaching out. Glad to be on your network.'

Start Engaging

You are now ready to start engaging. What are the opportunities out there to connect, converse and build your brand by communicating your expertise and thought leadership and revealing your talents and achievements?

- **Avenues for engaging**

  o **Share content**

    Use the LinkedIn 'Status Update' feature to share industry news, domain updates, interesting articles, personal achievements, professional events attended or organized as well as inspirational quotes and stories. Publish articles that demonstrate your domain knowledge and expertise on LinkedIn Pulse.

    Take care while curating your content and be mindful about what would appeal to your target audience and draw their interest and attention. Use rich media like videos and photos wherever possible to render your content more engaging.

  o **Respond to posts**

    Reviewing and responding to content posted by your network is as important as posting content yourself. Browse through the content and respond to it through a question, comment, like or reshare to start engagement.

    'After getting the feel of the platform in terms of the language and the rules of engagement, I moved on to sharing my ideas and posting content. I struck up conversations with a lot of people, reading their posts, commenting and asking questions,' says Abhijit Bhaduri about his engagement on Twitter. He explains,

    I met some interesting people along the way, with whom I made connections and built relationships. One such person is Bill Fischer. I chanced on a post in which William A. Fischer,

Professor of Innovation Management at IMD Business School at Lausanne, Switzerland, spoke about his book 'Reinventing Giants'. It drew my attention since innovation is an area of my interest and I started following Bill Fischer. One day Bill responded to a sketchnote that I had posted. This triggered a conversation and sometime later when Fischer was visiting Bangalore, we met in person, exchanging ideas over coffee.

Subsequently, Fischer invited Bhaduri to teach a class at IMD Lausanne and even wrote the foreword for Bhaduri's book—*The Digital Tsunami*. A casual connection thus developed into a friendship.

○ **Join relevant groups**

LinkedIn plays host to countless groups related to widely different domains and industries. Joining some of these relevant groups will not only enable you to broaden your network by connecting with industry peers but also keep you abreast of industry news and information. Engaging on these groups by voicing your opinions and participating in discussions is a great opportunity to establish your thought leadership, gain visibility and build your brand.

○ **Seek advocacy**

In addition to communicating your skills and achievements yourself, have others endorse you as a professional. It is not only easier but also more authentic and credible. LinkedIn provides two features to facilitate this.

▪ **Endorsement**

The endorsement section provides a generic list of skills that people can endorse you for. It would be judicious, however, to fine-tune this list, removing skills that you don't count as your core strengths or those not relevant in your current context and adding the ones that you would want to project and highlight for substantiating your brand and accomplishing your goals.

- **Recommendation**

    Anyone who has worked closely with you in some context, professionally or outside work—current and former colleagues, managers and clients—can recommend you through an example or a story, highlighting the skills, behaviour and traits that were manifested in the situation.

    People, however, may not be as forthcoming with recommendations as they may be with endorsements, as this calls for not just time, effort and writing skills but also staking their reputation and taking ownership of their advocacy.

    It would be prudent to curate a list of carefully selected people who know you well and write a personal note requesting them for a recommendation. Make it easy for them by stating the skills that you would like to be recommended for. Don't hesitate to follow-up after a decent interval because people have other more important matters to attend to and recommending you may not be high on their priority list.

    You could also engage in reverse promotion by taking the initiative to recommend someone, so people are encouraged to return the favour.

o **Other**

Take advantage of the notifications provided by LinkedIn on birthdays, work anniversaries or job movements of people in your network to wish people on their special days to generate more engagement.

- **Tone and flavour**

Purna Duggirala uses a casual and engaging style to carve out an informal, 'techy' persona consistent with the IT industry that he represents. This is reflected in the following elements across the length and breadth of his social media presence.

o *Name*—he has christened his portal 'Chandoo', his nickname.

o *Attire*—he is seen donning a casual T-shirt in his profile photos on all the social media channels.

o *Language*—his language is chatty, informal and flavoured with humour.

He shares personal anecdotes and family pictures on his website, allowing people a glimpse of the person he is behind the hardcore 'techy' exterior. For instance, he has shared the story about his transition from a corporate professional to an entrepreneur, along with the dilemmas he faced along the way. He presents his vulnerability before the audience when he states, 'I realized that I was a bad dad as I was not spending enough time with my kids.'

Abhijit Bhaduri's social media persona has an air of formality reflected both in his website and language aligned with the persona of seriousness of a prolific writer, who has authored books, reviewed books, music and movies, contributed articles to newspapers and magazines, often commenting on a range of subjects.

But he does reveal his lighter side with his brushes and sketch pens, which are his other constant companions besides the pen. A talented artist and cartoonist, he developed and mastered the technique of sketchnoting, taking cues from designer Mike Rohde, author of the bestselling book, *The Sketchnote Handbook.* Abhijit leverages this technique profusely, as he posts interesting, thought-provoking, colourful and visually appealing cartoons, water-colour sketches and photographs, commenting on leadership, workplace issues, personal effectiveness and current affairs. He has delighted people across social media channels like Instagram, LinkedIn and Twitter by presenting complex concepts and ideas in a simple, visually engaging format.

Chetna Vasishth dons a pleasant, warm and stylish demeanour in all her videos. She engages in simple and easy to understand English language which helps her connect with her audience comprising students not only in India but also in other countries.

Alok Jha prefers a casual and conversational persona in his videos. Hence, he records impromptu sans rehearsals.

It's important to be who you are and to align your tone and tenor with the brand that you are building. Genuineness and authenticity are critical.

- **Frequency of engagement**

  o Chetna Vasishth of ChetChat posts a video *every Friday* and she has done this over 200 times! 'To go through the cycle of releasing a video week after week—conceptualizing, storyboarding, shooting, editing, releasing and promoting —is a big task,' says Vasishth. 'It is akin to releasing a movie every week and demands such a gruelling schedule that sometimes I forget what it is like to chill over coffee with friends,' she says.

  o Alok Jha has posted close to 100 videos under the banner AJWednesday, expressing his thoughts and perspectives on a gamut of topics in the leadership, workplace and personal effectiveness space like growing and nurturing talent, connecting with people, celebrating successes, restraining attrition, leading a balanced life, engaging employees, the value of rejuvenation and the importance of a data-driven approach in HR. To post a video unfailingly *every Friday*, week after week calls for a very high degree of determination, persistence and tenacity.

o 'About 30–40 minutes a day is what it takes me to engage on the social media in a meaningful manner,' says Abhijit Bhaduri, who has 942 posts on his website and around 500 posts and sketchnotes on LinkedIn. He advises people to 'tweet as often as you eat' for an effective Twitter engagement.

o Similarly, during his tenure as the learning chief at Wipro, Bhaduri followed the practice of reaching out to 175,000 employees on a weekly basis, sharing relevant messages presented graphically using sketches and cartoon.

o Vijayraj Kamat spends time reading posts and browsing the social media every single day and posts content every one or two days.

o Chandoo engages several times a week on Twitter, posts a new video every week on YouTube, posts content once or twice a month on LinkedIn and comments and reacts to content posted by others multiple times a week. He has published thousands of posts, videos and podcasts on the social media.

Three insights emerge from this.

o **Regularity**

It is important to engage at a regular periodicity for making an impact and having people remember you and your message. Social media being a crowded place, people are grappling to be heard, and given the fact that people have short memories, they are likely to forget you if they don't see you or hear from you often enough.

It would be prudent to follow a structured approach to social media engagement by listing down your potential engagement activities, setting them to timelines, blocking some exclusive time for these activities on your calendar and then holding yourself accountable for timely execution.

o **Consistency**

- Chetna Vasishth provides career guidance to students and *all* her videos fall broadly within this domain.

- With a mission to 'Make you awesome in Excel' Chandoo constantly unravels the nuances of Excel to help people leverage the tool effectively in their business context, and his entire spectrum of social media engagement reflects this. Excel lies at the centre of all his posts.

- As an organizational development professional, Vijayraj Kamat writes and comments primarily on leadership and personal excellence.

- As an advisor to organizations on the future of work, talent and leadership, most of Abhijit Bhaduri's posts and comments are on the subjects of leadership, workplace excellence and personal effectiveness. Of course, he also tweets on topics as wide ranging as technology, design, films and books.

- Similarly, one of my industry colleagues writes and comments only on leadership. He has the knowledge and capacity to write on a host of other topics, but he chooses to write on leadership and leadership alone, both in print and the online media. This unwavering focus on leadership helps position him as a domain expert, with his name popping in the mind of anyone who is even remotely thinking of leadership. This is also reflected in the composition of his network which comprises leaders and people associated with leadership in some form or fashion.

While this is certainly a matter of choice, it is important to gain clarity around the brand that you are trying to devise and then orient your messaging strategy towards building and reinforcing that brand.

o **Patience**

Building a brand is a long haul that calls for a social media engagement marked by regularity and consistency, and this entails time, effort and patience. So, it is imperative that you strategize your social media activities to suit your goals, domain and schedule.

A Counterpoint

Madhu Khatri, former general counsel at Wipro and Microsoft, says,

Out of the total population of 7.5 billion, 3.5 billion are on social media today. There's a frenzy out there, noise, cacophony—a race to see and be seen, voicing, writing, blogging or creating other content. A brand, to my mind, is not defined by the number of articles, comments, connections and likes on social media. You need to identify your space, create your own world of influence comprising a group of people whom you know personally and professionally—business friends, colleagues and clients. My network comprises people who I know well, who I know will respond to my calls, people who have helped me and whom I have helped. That network is more important. It needs an investment of time & energy and at some level is selfless.

- Devise or revisit your social media engagement strategy.

- Review your profile and beef it up by leveraging the best practices discussed in this chapter, ensuring the presence of the following critical elements:

  o Profile photo

  o Background photo

  o Headline

  o Summary

  o Experience

- Review your network of connections.

  o Are the people in your ecosystem—current and former colleagues, clients, suppliers and other business partners—a part of your social media network? If not, reach out to them with invites.

  o Draw up a list of people who might be good to have on your network. Look for common connects for an introduction or reach out directly citing the context for the request.

  o Think of people you have been introduced to in the last couple of months and use your discretion to send them a connection invite.

- Identify appropriate social media channels.

- o Browse through the channels that you have identified and check out the rules of engagement.

- Engage
  - o Spend time browsing regularly and understand the rules of engagement of the particular channel.
  - o Start by responding to content posted by people in your network.
  - o List down the content that you could post based on your goals and set it to timelines.
  - o Join a few groups related to your industry or domain and start engaging on them.
  - o Seek endorsements and recommendations

- The social media offers a powerful platform to build your brand by assisting you in:
  - o Gaining visibility
  - o Getting recognition for your skills and expertise
  - o Building your network
  - o Expanding your knowledge and perspective
  - o Being abreast of current industry trends

- Leveraging the power of the social media calls for a carefully designed engagement strategy. Given below are the building blocks for curating a game plan for an effective social media engagement.

- **Prepare**
  - o Define your purpose.
  - o Choose the appropriate channels.
    - − Four channels stand out from a professional engagement standpoint—LinkedIn, Twitter, YouTube and Instagram.
  - o Post a powerful profile by logging all the critical elements like photo, background visual, headline, summary and work experience.
  - o Use the right keywords to facilitate LinkedIn and Google search.
  - o Leverage the principles of brevity and storytelling, and use an engaging style to generate interest.

- **Build your network**
  - o Start by inviting people in your ecosystem to join your network. Next, identify those who would be good to have. Seek an introduction from a common connect or request directly stating a context.
  - o This needs to be an ongoing activity.

- **Engage**
  - o Take care to understand the channel's rules of engagement.
  - o Spend time browsing through the content posted by people. Respond by liking, reposting and commenting on posts that resonate.
  - o Post content that demonstrates your expertise and intellectual capability.

- o Expand your network by joining groups related to your domain or industry. Participate in discussions to be recognized for your knowledge and perspective.

- o Seek advocacy by having people recommend you and endorse your skills.

- o Since people have short memories, it is important to engage frequently, regularly and with a consistent message in order to remain on their radar.

- o Be authentic and choose your language, tone and level of formality that is aligned with and reinforces your persona.

References

1. Rudyard Kipling. The elephant's child. In: Just so stories for little children [Internet]. 1902. Available from: http://pinkmonkey.com/dl/library1/kplng025.pdf
2. Gunaydin G, Selcuk E, Zayas V. Impressions based on a portrait predict, 1-month later, impressions following a live interaction. SAGE Publications [Internet]. 25 Aug 2016. Available from: https://journals.sagepub.com/doi/abs/10.1177/1948550616662123

05

Wrapping

The Fourth Dimension

Chapter 11

Making Your Wrapping Work

It is known that sales of tissues typically soar during the winter months and plummet in summer. Kleenex, a Kimberly–Clark brand that produces paper-based consumer products, including a variety of tissue papers, beat this trend in the summer of 2010, when they launched their product with an innovative and visually appealing packaging, structured in the form of slices of fruits like watermelon, orange and lime that are associated with sunny weather. The brand experienced almost a 100 per cent rise in sales due to the interest and intrigue triggered by the summer packaging design.[1]

'A retail package is the last and the best chance to make a sale,' says Marty Neumeier, author of *The Brand Gap*. With hundreds of products competing for attention on store shelves, packaging is, in fact, the last touch point in the marketing process that can sway purchase decisions. While logical factors like price and utility are at the core of the decision, emotions play an important role too.

The purchase decision is based on the way the buyer perceives the product in that moment—cool, elegant and affordable, or utilitarian, tacky, bulky and gauche? It is important to connect with the buyer at an emotional level, and the package design plays just as important a role in making this connection and influencing perceptions as the product itself.

A 2019 survey[2] of 250 brand owners across the consumer-packaged goods conducted by L.E.K. Consulting, a global strategy consulting firm, found that a whopping 75 per cent of the brand managers expected a rise in their packaging spend over the next one year, with nearly 33 per cent expecting more than a 10 per cent increase. What is the reason for this amplified emphasis on packaging? More than 90 per cent of the brand owners believed that packaging was a way to adapt to industry pressures and the constantly changing tastes and preferences of the consumer and, therefore, critical to their brand's success.

What holds for a product holds just as much for a person. Packaging matters.

Michael Burry, a Doctor of Medicine, had developed an interest in the financial markets very early in life. While pursuing his residency at the Stanford hospital, he decided to sidestep the field of medicine to launch a full-time career in the financial sector. He started a hedge fund called Scion Capital in 2000 and soon gained a formidable reputation as an investor. His hedge fund constantly beat the average market returns to produce mind-blowing profits for his investors, putting the spotlight on Burry and getting him instant recognition as one of the most discerning, perspicacious and shrewd hedge fund managers on Wall Street.

As deftly depicted in the 2015 film *The Big Short* based on Michaeal Lewis's book *The Big Short: Inside the Doomsday Machine*[3] about the run up of events that lead to the 2007–2008 financial crisis, Michael Burry was one of the first few people on Wall Street to comprehend the fault lines that lay beneath the sub-prime housing bubble. He had predicted that the bubble was waiting to burst, and it could happen as early as the second quarter of 2007. Based on this estimation, he had started betting long on the sub-prime housing market, when every other player in the market, riding high on the success of the sub-prime mortgage wave, was betting short.

Unfortunately, Michael Burry was unable to show the wisdom of his strategy to his investors, who brushed aside his claims about making a pot of money by betting long and demanded that he reverse his decision and sell. Confident in his knowledge and the merit of his prediction, when Burry refused to toe their line, they went up in arms and withdrew their money from his fund. As the financial meltdown played out in 2008 and the financial markets crashed around the world, the value of Burry's fund rocketed by 489 per cent, translating into a total profit of over $2.69 billion, proving the worthiness of his prediction beyond a speck of doubt.

However, in the aftermath of the crisis, when the financial market stakeholders got busy dissecting and piecing together the meltdown story, Burry, who was the first to foresee the crisis, and one of the very few to have actually made a fortune during this period, was conspicuously left out of all these discussions.

Why was Burry unable to convince the world about the efficacy of his prediction regarding the impending sub-prime housing market crisis? Why was he unable to persuade his investors to remain invested in his fund? After all, he had a compelling track record of sustained, 'higher than market' returns and the reputation of a knowledgeable, judicious and a very successful investor.

Michael Burry was undoubtedly brilliant, but he was idiosyncratic and unsocial.

While growing up, Burry had grievously injured an eye which had been replaced with an artificial glass eye. This very visible abnormality of eyes not moving in sync had impacted his ability to communicate. Coupled with this, he was also affected by a mild form of Asperger's syndrome, a neurodevelopmental disorder that makes social interaction and nonverbal communication considerably difficult. An awkward communicator thus, Burry was inept at socializing with people, to the extent that he was uncomfortable and gawky even when complimenting people. As a result, he had few friends at school, at university as well as at Wall Street.

He was idiosyncratic in other ways too. He was known to dress shabbily at work, often wearing the same T-shirt and shorts for days, walking shoeless and sleeping off in office at odd times, in sharp contrast to his other Wall Street colleagues, who evoked intrigue and epitomized professionalism in their dark suits, starched white shirts and visible social grace.

Burry's overall presentation and packaging was off-putting and fell far short of the eminence of his intellectual and functional capability, and this shortfall seriously assuaged his impact and influence with his stakeholders.

The importance of your wrapping—style, attire, demeanour and the way you communicate and carry yourself—in the context of your brand, is often underestimated. It tends to be looked upon as superficial and inconsequential, since it does not seem to be at the core of your assigned deliverables or goals. But your external wrapping can make a tremendous difference to the way you are perceived and the impact and influence that you wield.

It would be worthwhile to introspect and understand whether your wrapping is really worthy of your brand. Does it reinforce your brand, paving the way for your ideas to be heard? Is it supportive in establishing a positive emotional connect with your stakeholders, encouraging them to come forward and discover the value that resides within you, or does it distract them from getting through to the core to unravel your substance?

First Impressions

Observe the picture in Figure 11.1. What is your first impression? How do you perceive the person and why?

I have posed this question to more than a thousand people over the last few years and the typical responses that I have heard are—musician, junky, rock star, hippie, rogue, unkempt, untidy, dishevelled, calm and upset.

Jaron Zepel Lanier, portrayed in the picture, is in fact a writer, composer, visual artist, a computer scientist and a collector of rare musical instruments with an estimated net worth of $5 million. A pioneer in the field of virtual reality, Lanier founded VPL Research, one of the first companies to have developed and sold virtual reality products like goggles and gloves, in 1984. He has taught at various American universities and has worked as an interdisciplinary scientist at Microsoft Research.

How Are First Impressions Formed?

'We size up a person in a matter of seconds,' says Princeton psychologist Alexander Todorov, who conducted a research study along with Janine Willis, a student at the University. And in that

Figure 11.1.

Source: Alchetron. https://alchetron.com/Jaron-Lanier

fleeting moment, almost as a reflex action, we are quick to assess the person based on their facial expression, body language, attire and physical attributes such as weight and height, and our own worldview towards these attributes and, completely bypassing the rational thought process, even draw a judgment about the person's competence, trustworthiness and attractiveness. These impressions then colour our decisions and behaviour towards that person.[4]

People who perceived Jaron Zepel Lanier as a junky, hippie or a rogue, for instance, may take time and face some difficulty in discovering and responding to his immense intrinsic value and technical prowess when interacting with him or attending his class for the first time.

Similarly, people who stand tall are perceived as more intelligent, competent, authoritative and dominant and, therefore, better poise for leadership positions, compared with their more petite counterparts, putting them at a career advantage. This is corroborated by a study which found that 58 per cent of Fortune 500 CEOs are just shy of a height of six feet, while only 14.5 per cent of the male population is six feet or above.[5]

Another stereotype relates to overweight. Obese individuals are thought to be lazy and lacking in self-discipline. This could put them at a disadvantage compared with people with normal weight both for getting a job as well as the compensation that they command. Studies have shown that obesity lowered a man's annual earnings by an average of 2.3 per cent and those of a woman by as much as 4.5 per cent.

Daniel Selim Hamermesh, a noted economist and a professor of economics at Royal Holloway, University of London, explores the advantages of beauty in his book *Beauty Pays: Why Attractive People Are More Successful.* He shows how better-looking men and women have a distinct advantage at every juncture of life. For instance, attractive pupils receive better grades and attractive teachers better feedback from pupils. Similarly, attractive people are more likely to land that crucial first job, get a quicker promotion, a faster career progression and a higher pay, an advantage that their average-in-appearance colleagues, with similar qualification and experience, do not have.[6]

First impressions are also notoriously persistent—suggests a study by Bertram Gawronski, a social psychologist and professor of psychology at the University of Texas, and his team. Further, the first impression dominates regardless of how often it is contradicted by new experiences, unless it is challenged in multiple different contexts, at which point it may slowly lose its power.[7]

Since you can't change the way you look and have little control over your physical attributes such as height and weight, let's focus on factors that you do have control over, which contribute to a strong and compelling wrapping that helps generate a positive first impression, thus complementing and reinforcing your brand.

Dress with Care

Your Clothes Influence the Way You Are Perceived

In her bid to launch a career in journalism, Andrea Sachs, a fresh graduate from Northwestern University, lands a job at *Runway*, a high-end fashion magazine, in *The Devil Wears Prada*, the iconic comedy-drama film based on Lauren Weisberger's novel of the same name. She is tasked with assisting the high priestess of fashion and the editor-in-chief of the magazine, the very commanding and demanding, Miranda Priestly.

Walking into her new job, mocking at the frivolousness of the fashion industry, Sachs chooses to remain above that perceived superficiality, and this mindset manifests itself in various ways and most glaringly in her attire—prim, schoolgirl like and matter-of-factly—devoid of the slightest hint of style and quite skewed from the acceptable benchmarks of the fashion industry. Unsurprisingly, things don't go well for her as she's harassed and bullied by her boss.

Turning to the art director, Nigel, for advice, she learns that she needed to change her mindset. Rather than turning up her nose and holding herself above fashion, she needed to appreciate its relevance, embracing it in both word and spirit. On his advice, and with his support, Sachs takes the first step towards aligning with the world of fashion by changing her wardrobe and set eyes rolling and tongues wagging with a total image makeover. This not-so-subtle transformation does not go unnoticed by Priestly, who starts taking her more seriously and entrusting her with more responsibility.

The lesson? Presentation matters. Appearance matters. Wrapping matters.

At an event hosted by *Marie Claire*, an international monthly magazine that features a unique mix of style and substance, Sylvia Ann Hewlett, economist and the founding president of the Center for Work-Life Policy, a New York-based think tank that designs policies for enhancing work-life balance, aptly said, 'Appearance is an extraordinarily powerful first filtering. It can get you knocked off the list in a second. It is a crucial facet of executive presence.'[8]

Our choice of clothes has the power to influence the way people perceive us in ways that are hard to imagine. This is demonstrated by an interesting study conducted by Ben Fletcher, Head of the School of Psychology, University of Hertfordshire, along with Neil Howlett, Karen Pine and Ismail Orakcioglu.

In the study, 300 adults were shown the images of two men. In the first image, the model wore a custom-tailored suit, while in the second, he wore an off-the-shelf suit. The disparity between the suits was very subtle since the obvious differences like colour and design had been controlled. The faces in the two images had also been blurred to ensure that the facial expressions did not influence the impression. The study found that in just a three-second exposure, the man in the custom-tailored suit was judged more favourably on parameters like confidence, success and earning capacity.[9]

Attire Influences Your Own Thoughts and Actions

Evidently, our clothing plays a critical role in how people perceive our competence and intelligence.

Is the converse true as well? Can the clothes that we wear change our behaviour and the way we perceive the world? The answer, interestingly, is a categoric 'yes'.

'Enclothed cognition', a term coined by researchers Adam D. Galinsky and Hajo Adam, professor and assistant visiting professor, respectively, at the Kellogg School of Management at Northwestern University, refers to the influence that clothes have on the person's psychological process, and proposes that the clothes you wear directly affect the way you think and act. It is a subset of a broader field of study called 'embodied cognition', which postulates that humans 'think' both with their minds and bodies and that cognitive processes are deeply rooted in the body's interactions with the world.

Galinsky and Adam had conducted an experiment wherein 74 students were randomly assigned to two groups. People in both the groups were asked to don white coats over their normal clothes. The people in the first group were told that what they were wearing was a painter's coat, while those in the second group were told that they were wearing a doctor's coat. The two groups were subsequently put through brain games and mental agility tests.

It was found that the group where people thought that they wore the doctor's coat performed much better and showed far greater attention compared to the people in the other group. The symbolic power of the white coat apparently changed for people based on what it represented, and then wearing it made them more attentive or more artistic. This feeling then translated into actual changes not only in their behaviour but also their performance.[10]

Another study found a noteworthy correlation between formal attire and a person's thought process. 'Putting on formal clothes makes us feel powerful, and that changes the basic way we see the world,' says Abraham Rutchick, the author of the study and a professor of psychology at California State University, Northridge. Rutchick and his co-authors found that wearing formal clothing makes people think more broadly and holistically, rather than narrowly by getting into fine-grained details. In psychological parlance, wearing a suit encourages people to use abstract processing more readily than concrete processing.[11]

My own experience corroborates this. I have often found myself reaching out for a white shirt when dressing for an important meeting or presentation. A white shirt, I have noticed, boosts my confidence, paving the way for a superior engagement, speech or performance.

Similarly, ever thought about women's penchant for high-heeled shoes despite the obvious physical comfort? 'I can't do without heels. I think they add to my poise, stature and personality, imparting confidence and a sense of power,' was the response of one of my women colleagues. Interestingly, another colleague who is a leadership trainer, follows the somewhat outlandish practice of donning high-heeled shoes at the start of a program, when one requires maximum self-assurance to be able to establish one's credibility, subsequently changing into more comfortable shoes.

Attire Reinforces Your Brand

We have seen that clothes not only influence the way you are discerned by the world, they also influence your own mental make-up, thoughts and even actions. It is imperative, therefore, to select clothes with care, as they are crucial to your overall wrapping and image.

While a formal business attire is the norm in the financial world, especially for those in client servicing roles, media, advertising, entertainment and new-age industries like IT and e-commerce tend to have a more relaxed and casual dress code. It is advisable to broadly conform your clothing to the benchmarks of the industry that you represent.

Sumanto Chattopadhyay, Chairman and Chief Creative Officer of 82.5 Communications, Ogilvy Group, India, says,

I am often branded as the 'creative type' because the first thing that strikes a person about me is my long hair. I had grown my hair to perform Buddha's role in a play long ago, and have kept it like that ever since, as this also complements my casual way of dressing. I believe that I can come to work like this and get away with it because of the industry I am associated with. This persona may not have worked as well if I were working for a bank, for instance.

Similarly, Steve Jobs, the former CEO of Apple Inc. championed the turtleneck, jeans and sneakers, and Mark Zuckerberg, Chairman and CEO of Facebook, is usually seen in his customary grey T-shirt and hoody. This aligns well with the relative informality of the IT industry.

Stand out, while fitting in with your industry and company norms, therefore, is a useful mantra to bear in mind.

Make a Style Statement, but Dress to the Occasion

I heard the CEO of an engineering company say, 'Even during the pandemic induced lockdown days, when I was working from home, I took care to wear a formal suit during my conference calls with my clients as a mark of respect, even though the clients would invariably be casually dressed. This not only showed my seriousness towards the engagement, but also aligned with my personal brand.'

Mark Zuckerberg, too, is known to drop his usual grey T-shirt and hoody in favour of a formal suit and a tie when meeting heads of states.

India's Prime Minister, Narendra Modi's sartorial choices—impeccable, fashionable and carefully crafted—undoubtedly reinforce his image. He makes a style statement with his customary short-sleeved kurtas teamed with churidar pajamas and is known to change his attire as many as four times a day to present the perfect image befitting different occasions. Similarly, the late Indian politician Sushma Swaraj had established a saree along with a coordinated jacket as her trademark attire.

Accessorize Appropriately

Like your attire, accessories like make-up, bag, shoes, jewellery, belt, folder, pen, watch, diary and phone speak volumes about who you are and the professionalism you represent. Well-coordinated accessories in terms of colour, shape and size enhance the persona, point to your attention to detail, taste and style and go a long way in either complementing and fortifying your brand or weakening it.

I once went for a meeting at a financial services company with a colleague who exuded confidence in a dark suit teamed with a pair of red stilettos and a branded red bag. I thought that was chic, even bold, and marvelled at her ability to carry it with panache. But during the meeting, I noticed that the client was visibly uncomfortable and distracted. The same boldly accessorized outfit may have worked better with a different audience. Accessories, thus, should be subtle, complementing and enhancing. They should work towards enhancing the image without distracting the audience from your core message.

Dress for the Next Level

A former colleague at a company that advocated an informal dress code, except for those in client-facing roles, showed courage in following the practice of donning a tie to office, when no one else in the office, including his senior stakeholders, wore ties.

How did this impact him? It helped him create a persona that spelt confidence and seniority. People took notice and looked up to him, as he stood out from the pack, perceiving him as a senior member of the team. He was soon promoted to the next level, since this persona was also matched by stellar performance.

Play by the Rules

I remember inviting a trainer from Kolkata to deliver a session on a niche technology, and people just loved his sessions since his technical skills were beyond compare. Following my customary practice, I invited him for lunch at the cafeteria in a bid to strike a personal rapport. And then something queer happened. When I raised my eyes to look up to respond to something he had just said, I encountered the most discomfiting sight in his manner of eating. Disgusted, I found it difficult to push food down my throat. Thereafter, while I continued inviting him for the training sessions, I refrained from inviting him for lunch.

Another time, I was disconcerted when a participant walked into my training session chewing betel leaves. Perceiving this act as incongruent with the generally accepted decorum of the corporate world, my unconscious bias kicked in quickly, triggering an instant aversion, which even caused me to rubbish his competence. It was only much later during my conversation with the program sponsors that I learnt that this person was, in fact, the company's best-performing salesperson, and the company was currently investing in coaching him to let go of his betel-leaf-chewing habit.

Similarly, several IT professionals are known for being sent back from onsite projects, not for want of technical skills but for reasons related to their wrapping in terms of hygiene, attire and manners. Their inability to project a persona that befitted their own personal, as well as the company's brand, proved to be their nemesis.

Your wrapping, thus, transcends a wide spectrum of elements like attire, etiquette, communication style and even the way you keep your desk, as people form impressions about you based on this. While a cluttered desk gives an impression of being chaotic, spelling oversights point to inattention or carelessness, and failing to return a call or acknowledge an email suggest a lack of etiquette and sensitivity.

Introduce Yourself Effectively

One is often called upon to introduce oneself on various occasions —conferences, seminars, meetings, training programs and social and business parties. How often have you made an impact and got people interested by introducing yourself in a way that is worthy of you? There have been occasions when I have overlooked important headlines, not used the right words, or not communicated eloquently enough when introducing myself. And then, dissatisfied, I have inwardly reprimanded myself for doing injustice to who I really am. The way you introduce yourself can help establish a positive first impression, thereby enhancing your wrapping and reinforcing your brand.

Be Prepared

The trick for representing yourself in a way that becomes you lies in careful preparation. Follow these three useful steps:

- Write down your headlines or your unique value proposition.
- Write down a few important details around each headline. Quantify these details wherever possible.
- Weave a narrative around it.

Here's an example.

The headlines:

- Corporate career in HR
- Freelance trainer, facilitator and coach
- Columnist—contributing articles to newspapers
- Engagement with the academia—visiting faculty at business schools
- Education and certification

The details:

- Corporate career in HR
  - o More than 25 years, organizations worked at and roles played
- Freelance trainer, facilitator and coach
  - o Areas of training and coaching and organizations engaged with
- Columnist—contributing articles to newspapers
  - o Types of articles and newspapers written for
- Academia—visiting faculty at business schools
  - o Names of schools and subjects taught
- Education and certification
  - o Degrees and certificates

The narrative:

I am a trainer, facilitator, coach and a columnist.

After a corporate career in HR at Morgan Stanley, Capgemini, Datamatics and NIIT, I shifted gears in 2012 to start Delta Learning, an HR consulting and training company.

I have trained and coached individuals and teams in more than 55 companies across 6 industries in the areas of leadership, professional skills and diversity. I have engaged with teams at Bank of America, ANZ, HDFC Bank, Deutsche Bank, Capgemini, Larsen & Toubro, Future Generali among others.

I write on leadership, workplace excellence and diversity and have more than 55 published articles in *Mint, Financial Express, Business Standard, Economic Time* and other publications.

I am an alumna of Delhi School of Economics, am certified on DISC and Oscar Murphy's battery[5] and a visiting faculty at Narsee Monjee Institute of Management Studies, S. P. Jain Institute of Management and Research and National Institute of Securities Markets.

Note the use of data to indicate depth.

- 55 companies across 6 industries

- 55 published articles

Be Audience-centric

Audience-centricity is the key. The above narrative will work when, for example, I am introducing myself to an HR head of an organization. But it needs to be tailored to the needs of other audiences. Here are three examples of how the introduction can be customized based on the audience.

Audience—Relatives and friends who may not be familiar with corporate jargon:

'I coach people on how to write and speak with their clients, colleagues and bosses effectively. I work with both organizations and individuals.'

Audience—Editor of a newspaper with whom I am exploring opportunities for writing:

'I am a trainer, facilitator, coach and a columnist. After a corporate career in HR at Morgan Stanley, Capgemini, Datamatics and NIIT, I now run Delta Learning, an HR consulting and training company.'

'I have been writing on leadership, personal effectiveness and diversity for more than a decade. I have more than 55 published articles in *Mint, The Financial Express, Business Standard, The Economic Times* and other publications.'

'Most of my other work is in the area of people development—I coach and train people, working with both organizations and individuals.'

Audience—Educational institution where I am exploring teaching opportunities:

'I am a trainer, facilitator, coach and a columnist. After a corporate career in HR at Morgan Stanley, Capgemini, Datamatics and NIIT, I now run Delta Learning, an HR consulting and training company.'

'I have taught more than 3,000 students at Narsee Monjee Institute of Management Studies, S. P. Jain Institute of Management and Research and National Institute of Securities Markets in the capacity of visiting faculty. I have taught business communication and the learning and development paper to MBA students.'

'The majority of my work is with corporate clients, having engaged with teams at more than 55 companies across 6 industries in the areas of leadership, professional skills and diversity. My clients include Bank of America, ANZ, HDFC Bank, Deutsche Bank, Capgemini, Larsen & Toubro and Future Generali among others.'

'I write on leadership, personal effectiveness and diversity and have more than 55 published articles in the *Mint, Financial Express, Business Standard, Economic Times* and other publications.'

Be Distinctive

Consider this scenario—'The global operations head of a multinational bank was slated to meet the operations team at Mumbai on her recent visit to India. The team, comprising 10 members, was asked to introduce itself to the visiting practice head.'

I had asked the participants in a training session at a multinational bank to respond to the above scenario. 10 people introduced themselves, all roughly echoing the following.

'Hi, I am Ranjini. I am a computer science engineer and I have been with the bank for more than eight years. I have worked on three different processes during the last five years. I am conversant with Python and I currently support the business finance and the CFO team on financial and management reporting and analytics.'

The practice head is likely not to remember anyone, since there is nothing distinctive that differentiates this person's introduction from that of the others. Again, in the spirit of audience-centricity, ask yourself:

- What would the practice head like to hear?
- What does she know already?
- What can I say that would be distinctive and would help me stand out from the rest of the pack?

Include the following:

- Any achievements you may have to bring about efficiencies and cost reduction.
- Any evidence of cross-functional knowledge and experience.
- Any evidence of contribution and achievements beyond your role definition. For example, participation in volunteering activity, hosting events, leading cross-functional projects.

- Any personal interests and achievements. These may stick in the mind and hold you apart just like your professional achievements.

Importantly, customize your introduction to include things which this person may appreciate. It may, therefore, be helpful to read the profile of the person to understand their areas of interest and what they care about. For instance, if you have figured that they care about volunteering and that they oversee volunteering initiatives in the global operations practice, talk about it, if you have volunteered.

Let's incorporate these elements in the introduction.

Example 1

Hi, I am Ranjini, I am a computer science engineer, have worked with the bank for eight years, worked on three different processes and am conversant with Python like most of my colleagues here.

My team has automated two processes in the last two months, reducing the processing time by more than 10 seconds per transaction. This translates to a reduction in processing time to the extent of 30 mins per day and 11 hours per month.

I lead the bank's 'one person, one plant' campaign in Mumbai and I am a trained Kathak dancer.

Example 2

Hi, I am Ranjini. I am a computer science engineer and have had the novel experience of moving across different processes every one of the six years that I have been with the bank. This has given me the unique opportunity to learn and be conversant with six different processes.

I love teaching and have put in 35 hours of process training across four teams over and above my regular work. Currently,

I am taking some online courses and aiming for certification in AI programming language, Lisp, since we are slated to use this in one of our upcoming projects.

I enjoy watching Hollywood movies in my spare time. In fact, I would call myself a movie buff.

Be Well Rehearsed

Remember that practice sits between a good and a great introduction. So, practice your introduction to internalize the keywords and data points, so that these trip off your tongue easily when you are on stage. Practice standing (or sitting) tall, looking people in the eye and engaging with a smile. This investment of time will enable you to articulate your content smoothly, confidently and impactfully.

- Observe the wrapping donned by your role model in terms of attire, accessories and mannerisms.

  o Identify five areas where you think you would like to enhance your own wrapping in the context of these observations.

  o What actions will you take to bring about these changes?

- Write down your self-introduction tailored to the following scenarios:

  o You are attending a conference where the delegates are asked to introduce themselves. The delegates are your industry colleagues.

  o The newly appointed CEO is meeting your team and each team member has been asked to introduce themselves.

o   You are interviewing for a job role.

- Wrapping, the outmost layer of your brand, transcends your attire and the way you carry yourself and communicate.

- It is important to sport an attractive wrapping that encourages people to discover and appreciate your intrinsic value, for your strengths may never be appreciated if they are hidden under a clumsy exterior.

- Studies show that people form snap judgments about your competence, intelligence and confidence based on your external wrapping and this is the filter through which all your subsequent actions are viewed.

- Clothing, an important element of your wrapping, not only plays a critical role in how you are perceived by others, it also has the power to change the way you think, act and perceive the world. Consider the following points when selecting your attire:

  o   Align with your industry

  o   Dress to the occasion

  o   Dress for the next level

  o   Accessorize appropriately

- Make a great first impression by introducing yourself impactfully. Craft a compelling self-introduction by:

  o   Being prepared

  o   Being audience-centric

  o   Being distinctive

  o   Being well rehearsed

References

1. Newman AA. A sharp focus on design when the package is part of the product. The New York Times [Internet]. 8 July 2010. Available from: https://www.nytimes.com/2010/07/09/business/media/09adco.html

2. L.E.K. Consulting. Huge percentage of brand owners will spend more on packaging, finds new study. Cision PR Newswire [Internet]. 8 May 2019. Available from: https://www.prnewswire.com/news-releases/huge-percentage-of-brand-owners-will-spend-more-on-packaging-finds-new-study-300845887.html

3. Lewis M. The big short: inside the doomsday machine. New York: W. W. Norton & Company; 2010.

4. Boutin C. Snap judgments decide a face's character, psychologist finds. Princeton University [Internet]. 22 Aug 2006. Available from: https://www.princeton.edu/news/2006/08/22/snap-judgments-decide-faces-character-psychologist-finds#:~:text=Todorov%20and%20co%2Dauthor%20Janine,of%20the%20journal%20Psychological%20Science.

5. Timothy A, Cable DM. The effect of physical height on workplace success and income: preliminary test of a theoretical model. J Appl Psychol [Internet]. 2004; 89(3): 428–441. Available from: https://www.princeton.edu/news/2006/08/22/snap-judgments-decide-faces-character-psychologist-finds#:~:text=Todorov%20and%20co%2Dauthor%20Janine,of%20the%20journal%20Psychological%20Science.

6. Hamermesh DS. Beauty pays: why attractive people are more successful. Princeton, NJ: Princeton University Press; 2 Aug 2011.

7. Gawronski B, Rydell RJ, Vervliet B, Houwer JD. Why first impressions are so persistent. J Exp Psychol: General [Internet]. 2010;139(4):683. DOI: 10.1037/a0020315. Available from: https://www.sciencedaily.com/releases/2011/01/110118113445.htm

8. Marie Claire [Internet]. Do you have executive presence? Available from: https://www.marieclaire.com/career-advice/tips/a7342/do-you-have-executive-presence/

9. Fletcher BC. What your clothes might be saying about you. Psychology Today [Internet]. Available from: https://www.psychologytoday.com/intl/blog/do-something-different/201304/what-your-clothes-might-be-saying-about-you

10. Adam H, Galinsky AD. Enclothed cognition. J Exp Soc Psychol [Internet]. Jul 2012;48(4):918–25. Available from: http://www.utstat.utoronto.ca/reid/sta2201s/2012/labcoatarticle.pdf

11. Slepian ML, Ferber SN, Gold JM, Rutchick AM. The cognitive consequences of formal clothing. Soc Psychol Personal Sci [Internet]. 2015;6(6):661–668. Available from: http://www.columbia.edu/~ms4992/Publications/2015_Slepian-Ferber-Gold-Rutchick_Clothing-Formality_SPPS.pdf

Chapter 12

Speak Your Brand

The 2010 historical drama film, *The King's Speech*, written by David Seidler and directed by Tom Hooper, poignantly depicts the pain, embarrassment and humiliation of Prince Albert, the future king of England, when he falters and fumbles through his ineloquent speech at the British Empire Exhibition at Wembley in 1925. His powerful brand embodying his intellect, his perfect appearance and manners, as well as his stellar lineage, come to a naught for lack of oratory skills that emanated from a debilitating stammer. The film traces his painful and arduous journey for overcoming this disability with the support of speech therapist Lionel Logue. Their efforts bear fruit when he overcomes his stammer successfully and gives an impassioned and inspiring speech, befitting a king, at the onset of the Second World War in September 1939.

Your ability to be heard and get your ideas across, have people take notice and influence an audience, is evidently critical for success.

It rests on the twin pillars of, first, your credibility, which stems from your personal, relational and positional power and, second, your communication skills. This is inarguably an important dimension of your wrapping and an essential component of your brand.

Here are six principles for communicating powerfully.

1. Begin with a punch

Remember that in an attention-deficit and distracted world, the first 60 seconds are critical in grabbing the attention of the audience, establishing your credibility and setting off to a stimulating start. Therefore, don't fritter away these precious moments thanking people, communicating boring housekeeping items or rambling around an obvious agenda. Instead, communicate the headlines of your message and get the audience instantly interested and motivated to listen by kickstarting with an attention-seizing story, video, quote, question or data. Consider the following examples.

• **Starting with a question**

When speaking on the *business case for gender diversity*, for instance, get the audience instantly involved by asking:

o How did the workforce participation rate of women in India change between 2000 and 2019?

• **Revealing startling data**

Share the following data to have the audience instantly sit up in their chairs:

o The workforce participation rate of women in India *declined* from 30.4 per cent in 2000 to 23.4 per cent in 2019.

o At 23 per cent, India is at par with Saudi Arabia and behind Pakistan (24%) and Sri Lanka (35%).[1]

- **Starting with a story**

Get people interested by introducing the topic 'Leaders Need to Walk the Talk' through this story:

Paul Anderson took charge of BHP Limited, a leading global resources company, in 1998 when projects were failing, the share price was at an all-time low and people were demotivated.

Anderson implemented a turn-around strategy, taking some hard decisions along the way and instilling trust by taking people into confidence and leveraging the combined wisdom of his team. The success of the strategy was evident when the company posted its highest ever profit of $1.6 billion in 2000. All other performance parameters also looked northward, barring one—safety. This was discouraging both from the people's morale as well as the company reputation perspective.

When questioned by Anderson, the head of safety rightly said that people tend to take cues from and model their behaviour around what they see at the top.

People have seen their CEO riding his motorcycle without a helmet and exceeding the prescribed speed limit of 5 miles per hour while driving on campus. Moreover, when visiting the plants you don't necessarily wear the recommended safety gear and when speaking with your management team, safety is perhaps the last item that you speak about.

Anderson got the message. He mended his ways which, coupled with a few more measures, institutionalized and built a culture of safety, pushing this parameter northward as well.

It is imperative, therefore, for leaders to demonstrate behaviours that they advocate.

2. Leverage the power of three

Ever wondered why the number three is omnipresent?

- In timeless tales such as:
  - The Three Musketeers
  - Three Little Pigs
  - Goldilocks and the Three Bears
- In eternal quotes such as:
  - I came, I saw, I conquered
  - Friends, Romans and countrymen
  - A government of the people, for the people, by the people
- In phrases such as:
  - The Father, the Son and the Holy Spirit
  - Ready, steady, go
  - The sun, the moon and the stars

Notice the repeated references of *three* elements in the following excerpt from President Barack Obama's re-election victory speech given in Chicago in 2012.

> ***Thank you for believing all the way, through every hill, through every valley.***
>
> ***You'll hear the determination in the voice of a young field organizer...***
>
> ***You'll hear the pride in the voice of a volunteer...***
>
> ***You'll hear the deep patriotism in the voice of a military spouse...***
>
> ***That's why we do this. That's what politics can be. That's why elections matter.***

It's not small. It's big. It's important.

We believe in a generous America, in a compassionate America, in a tolerant America.

America, I believe we can build on the progress...

I believe we can keep the promise of our founders...

I believe we can seize this future together....

- **What's so magical about three? Why three?**

It is said that once is an accident, twice a coincidence and three times a pattern. Our brain is tuned to recognizing patterns— patterns of objects, facts, ideas, emotions and people. And three is the smallest quantum of information that forms a rhythm or a pattern. Elements grouped in three, therefore, are more rhythmical, more memorable and more digestible because of the way our brain is programmed.

What does this mean in the context of communication?

- **Structure your message in three parts**

Leverage the power of three by using three sections to structure your message as demonstrated in the examples below.

o   Beginning, middle, end

o   Problem, cause, solution

o   Past, present, future

o   What, why, how

o   Current reality, challenge, resolution

- **Present three arguments**

Make three points, present three main ideas or outline three steps. Don't overwhelm your audience by communicating 8 or 15. Consider the examples below.

- Question: Why should we hire you?

- Answer: There are three main reasons I believe I would be a good fit for this job role:

  - *First,* my pertinent work experience

  - *Second,* my track record

  - *Third,* my ability to collaborate and work under pressure.

- Question: What factors have led to your organization's success?

- Answer: I believe there are three factors that form the cornerstone of our success:

  - *One,* our customer first policy

  - *Two,* our compelling HR practices

  - *Three,* our emphasis on innovation.

- **Split your content in smaller nuggets, but stick to three**

  When you have a lot of information, break it up into smaller chunks as depicted in Figures 12.1 and 12.2.

Figure 12.1.

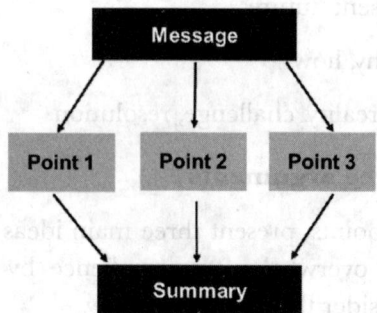

Figure 12.2.

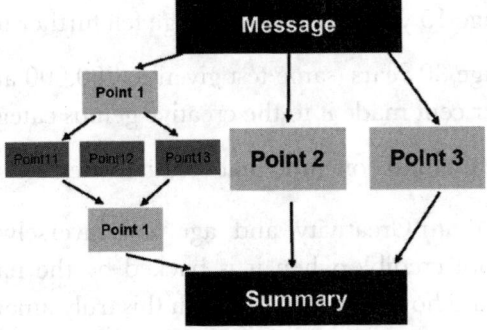

Thus, render your message more impactful and memorable for your audience by leveraging the power of three.

3. Quote a credible source

Consider this example.

'Creativity and age are inversely correlated.'

I have seen people regard this statement with a fair degree of scepticism. But people take notice and see the truth in the statement when I put the following narrative around it.

Creativity researchers George Land and Beth Jarman did an interesting study in 1968, later published in their book *Breakpoint and Beyond: Mastering the Future Today*, to determine whether there is any correlation between creativity and age. They administered a test that they had earlier devised and successfully used to recruit innovative engineers and scientists at NASA, to 1,600 children in the age group of three to five years. They went on to retest the same group of children at age 10 and 15 years and came up with some astounding results. The research found that:

- At age 3 to 5 years—98 per cent of the children scored the creative genius category

- At age 10 years—the percentage fell to 30

- At age 15 years—the percentage fell further to 12

- At age 30 years (same test given to 280,000 adults)—only 2 per cent made it to the creative genius category

This led them to conclude that creativity declines with age.[2]

The claim that 'Creativity and age are inversely correlated' becomes more credible when it is backed by the names of the researchers and how they came up with this truly amazing insight.

Here's another example.

> Frontline managers are the backbone of an organization and critical to its success. Organizations would be do well to invest in the development of this important cohort as their effectiveness impacts business performance.

The same statement becomes more impactful when it is backed by a reliable source.

> In her book, *Becoming a Manager: How New Managers Master the Challenges of Leadership,* the Wallace Brett Donham professor of business administration at Harvard Business School Linda A. Hill, writes, 'Managers on the front line are critical to sustaining quality, service, innovation, and financial performance.'[3]

> In a survey done by the Harvard Business Review Analytic Services to understand the role of frontline managers in the organization's success, 77 per cent of the respondents said that frontline managers are critical for helping their organization reach its business goals, but only 33 per cent felt that their organization's frontline managers were competent in business-based decision-making, while only 12 per cent said that their organization was currently investing sufficiently in the development of frontline managers.[4]

Backing your statement with a credible source thus eliminates any trace of cynicism that the audience might be nursing.

4. Appeal to logic *and* emotion

Wearing a seat belt is imperative for ensuring safety.

Data suggests that:

- People without seat belts are 30 times more likely to be ejected from a vehicle during a crash.

- More than three out of four people who eject die from injuries.

- A whopping 75 per cent passenger vehicle users in India don't wear seat belts, leading to 15 deaths every day.

This narrative, wrapped in strong and credible data takes a rational, cognitive route, but there is a slim chance that it will drive people to action as it misses emotional appeal.

Consider an alternative narrative below:

My friend, Rameshwari, shared her nightmarish, near death, experience the other day.

'I was driving to Pune last weekend to see my mother. I was enjoying the drive, going at an easy pace and listening to my favourite Yanni songs. I jumped out of my skin when I suddenly heard a big bang and the screeching of tyres! Hit by a lorry, my car skidded from the highway, swirling, bouncing and crashing 30 feet down into the fields. I shut my eyes tightly waiting for imminent death. A few seconds later, completely shaken, I looked up from the corner of my eye and realized that I was hanging in an upside-down position on my seat belt. I clicked the seat belt open and slowly crawled out of the car through the passenger window. It was miraculous that

I got away with just a few broken bones. I attribute my life completely to the seat belt which I had thankfully remembered to put on that fateful day,' she said.

A seat belt is, indeed, the only saviour in the event of a crash. People without seat belts are 30 times more likely to be ejected from a vehicle during a crash and three out of four people who are ejected die from their injuries.

This narrative is woven around a story and fortified with facts. By outlining characters, their challenges and the actions taken to overcome the challenges, stories serve the twin purpose of capturing the attention of the audience as well as establishing an emotional connect. Cognitive psychologist Jerome Bruner says that a fact wrapped in a story is 22 times more memorable. In fact, humans love stories as our brains are hardwired for them.

Here's another example.

In her famous, 10,412,544 times viewed TED Talk, 'Why We Have Too Few Women Leaders', one of the points Sheryl Sandberg, the COO of Facebook, makes is that women systematically underestimate their own abilities.[5]

'If you test men and women, and you ask them questions on totally objective criteria like GPAs, men get it wrong slightly high, and women get it wrong slightly low,' she says.

But Sandberg does not stop here. The audience listens with rapture as she elaborates the point with a story.

When I was in college, my senior year, I took a course called European Intellectual History. And I took it with my roommate, Carrie, who was then a brilliant literary student—and went on to be a brilliant literary scholar—and my brother—smart guy, but a water-polo-playing pre-med, who was a sophomore. The three of us take this class together. And then Carrie reads all the books in the original Greek and Latin, goes to all the lectures. *I read all the books in English and go to most of the lectures. My brother is kind of busy. He reads one book and goes to a couple of lectures, marches himself up to our room a couple days before the exam to get himself tutored. The three of us go to the exam together. And we sit there for three hours. We walk out, we look at each other, and we say, 'How did you do?' And Carrie says, 'Boy, I feel like I didn't really draw out the main point on the Hegelian dialectic.' And I say, 'God, I really wish I had really connected John Locke's theory of property with the philosophers that follow.' And my brother says, 'I got the top grade in the class'.*

You got the top grade in the class? You don't know anything!

Consider this example:

The customer is very powerful today as they have greater choices, are very well informed and have a strong voice owing to the social media.

This is like stating the obvious, but notice the spike in your interest when this point is demonstrated with a story.

When Dave Carroll, a Canadian musician and songwriter, was waiting to board a United Airlines plane along with his band, on a week-long-tour of Nebraska, he was horrified to see the baggage handlers chuck the bags around with utter disregard. He reached out to the flight attendant to draw her attention to the scene playing out outside. She, however, didn't sound too concerned and directed him instead to the lead agent outside. When he reached out to the lead agent, he disappeared into the crowd saying that he was only the 'acting' lead agent and directed him to someone else.

Upon reaching his destination, his concerns proved to be true when he found that his guitar had been badly damaged.

Three days later, after concluding his concerts, when he put in his damage claim at the United Airlines office, he was utterly taken aback when he was told that the claim could not be considered because, as per policy, such claims should be handed in within 24 hours of travel. Dave then ran from pillar to post, taking his case to all and sundry, including the CEO, but to no avail.

Finally, utterly frustrated, he vented out his experience in a song called *United breaks guitars* and posted it on YouTube, not really thinking that it would attract much attention. But to his utter delight, the video went viral with over 1 million views in a matter of just three days, bringing United Airlines to its feet, which changed its baggage claim policy with immediate effect.

The customer is, indeed, powerful today as they have greater choices, are very well informed and have a strong voice owing to the social media.

5. Use imagery to bring your narrative to life

Imagery refers to the visually descriptive language comprising metaphors and similes. Like stories and pictures, imagery helps conjure up vivid images in the mind of the reader or the listener, making the narrative more real and leading to greater interest and involvement.

Here are a few examples.

- **The peanut butter manifesto**

Brad Garlinghouse, a senior vice president at Yahoo, (currently CEO of Ripple), realized that all was not well at the company. But unlike others, who chose to let things go by, Garlinghouse decided to outline his perception of what was ailing the company, coupled with a strategy to bring it back on track, in an internal manifesto in 2006. The manifesto was later published in the Wall Street Journal.

'We lack a focused, cohesive vision for our company. We want to do everything and be everything—to everyone,' he wrote. 'There are so many people in charge (or believe that they are in charge) that it's not clear if anyone is in charge,' he added.

The manifesto was peppered with references to peanut butter, which Garlinghouse uses to show how the company had been rendered ineffective by spreading itself too thin, making a foray into a wide range of new businesses. He called for a structural reorganization with a 20 per cent cut in its workforce.

'I hate peanut butter. We all should,' he concluded.

This constant allusion to peanut butter caught people's attention and the manifesto came to be known as 'the peanut butter manifesto'.

- **Providing a restaurant experience**

In the early 1990s, in a bid to make computers easier to use and render them more accessible to people, product managers Karen Fries and Barry Linnet at Microsoft advocated the launch of a software with a social interface incorporating cartoon characters which would guide the users and help them achieve their computing tasks.

Their pitch, woven around a rational, cognitive argument, comprised a prototype that demonstrated their understanding of this new technology, a market research report that pointed to an encouraging response from end users, an endorsement from two Stanford University Professors, Clifford Nasa and Byron Reeves, who were experts in human–computer interaction, coupled with sound financial projections and the first-mover advantage.

Additionally, they used imagery, appealing to the right brain and evoking the listener's imagination to reinforce their message. Using the experience of having a meal as an analogy, they said that to cook a meal, you would first look for a recipe, then go to the nearest supermarket and scurry around the racks to pick up the ingredients, all of which may not be available in a single place.

'At Microsoft we have been providing our customers the supermarket experience all these years,' they said. 'We are proposing that the time is ripe to enhance that experience by providing a restaurant-like set up, wherein instead of going through the rigmarole of cooking a meal at home, people have the option of driving to a restaurant, selecting the dishes of their choice from the menu, enjoying the ambience and engaging in a conversation while the dishes are cooked behind the scene, paying up and driving back,' they added.

6. Use the right language

Sometimes, a well-intended conversation initiated in a sensitive context like managing performance or resolving a conflict may fall short of yielding the desired result in the absence of appropriate language.

Consider this comment: 'Your presentation was not up to the mark.'

Ambiguous and critical statements like these strike at the person, not behaviour or performance. The words 'not up to the mark' communicate that something is amiss, without really clarifying what exactly needs to change. Moreover, being evaluative and judgmental, the words are likely to turn the person defensive and lead to a debate or argument.

The same message could have been delivered in a way that the person emerges from the dialogue feeling positive.

- I want to talk to you about your presentation at the monthly meeting yesterday. It appeared to me that you were uncertain about the sales numbers you had quoted, and your revenue calculations too were incorrect. (State the facts clearly sans judgment.)

- I felt uncomfortable because the entire senior management team was present. I'm worried that this might impact your image and the reputation of our team. (State the impact.)

- How do you think you could address this? What are your thoughts around this? Is there something I could do to help? (Ask for views and determine cause.)

- So, we agree that you will take these actions.... (Conclude with an action plan.)

The following communication rules emerge from this example.

- **Be specific**
  o Your performance needs improvement.
    - Define 'improvement'. State your observations which have led you to think that the performance is short of expectations.

      'You were uncertain about the sales numbers you had quoted and your revenue calculations too were incorrect.'
  o You are always late.
    - State the number of times the person has been late to avoid any debate or argument.

'Last month you were late eight times.' This statement leaves no room for debate.

- **Separate facts from interpretation**
  - You were not attentive during the meeting.
    - Your conclusion about the person being inattentive must be based on certain observations. State your observations first.

      'I observed that you were rolling your eyes and looking out of the window when the other team members were talking in the meeting.'

  - You are trying to sideline me.
    - State the facts that suggested that the person was trying to sideline you.

      'I have noticed that you set up our last two team meetings without consulting me and you did not include me in your meeting with the general manager.'

- **State your interpretation tentatively**

  While facts cannot be refuted, your interpretation can. Therefore, state the facts directly and your interpretation tentatively, thereby acknowledging that there could be a chance that you may have missed something and your openness to hearing the other side of the story.

  - You were not attentive in the meeting.
    - 'I observed that you were rolling your eyes and looking out of the window when the other team members were talking in the meeting. *This gave me a sense that you may not be fully present in the meeting.'*

  - You are trying to sideline me.

- 'I have noticed that you set up our last two team meetings without consulting me and you did not include me in your meeting with the general manager. *This tends to make me feel that I am being sidelined.*'

o This suggests that you are not doing your share of work.

- 'This gives me a sense that you may not be doing your share of the work.'

o You have not understood the situation.

- 'I get a feeling that you may not have understood the situation completely.'

- **Use the 'I' language**

Consider this statement: 'You did not bother to inform me.'

The word 'you' sounds accusatory and is akin to pointing a finger which may not go down well with the person. Instead try using the 'I' language. Using 'I' instead of 'you', strips the message off its accusatory element, rendering the message more acceptable to the listener.

o You did not bother to inform me.

I was waiting to hear from you.

o You did not consult me on the timing and agenda.

I was not consulted on the timing and agenda.

o I called you a couple of times, but you did not return my call.

I called you a couple of times, but I did not hear back from you.

o You went for lunch without me.

I was hoping to join you for lunch yesterday.

- **Use these conversation starters**

  Sometimes, it is difficult to find the right words to start a difficult conversation. Consider using the conversation starters below.

  o   I'd like to talk to you about an important concern.

  o   I want to share my concerns about our project.

  o   I want to share my feelings about what happened at the meeting yesterday.

- **Invite the other person's perspective**

  o   I'd really like to hear your opinion on this.

  o   Please let me know if you see things differently.'

  o   I want to hear your thoughts.

  o   Am I missing something?

  o   Can you explain your thought process, so I understand where you are coming from?

  o   Can you help me understand the way you are seeing things?

It is important, therefore, to engage in a constructive dialogue, using the right words to drawing attention towards specific behaviours or performance elements that need adjustment, with a spirit of facilitating a change, rather than punishing or threatening.

Just as subconsciously we consider labels and wrappers in estimating a product's worth, people experience us first by their sense of sight, before deep diving to discover our inherent worth. Your wrapping, encompassing the way you dress, communicate and present yourself, in general, is undoubtedly a significant part of your identity and crucial to the way you are perceived and judged, no matter where you work and what you do. Your substance may be rendered worthless and your strengths unacknowledged, if they are hidden under a clumsy or unattractive packaging that dissuades people from accessing it.

- Seek feedback from your mentor or anyone else whom you trust on the way you communicate in different contexts. Draw up an action plan to work on the feedback received.

- Your ability to influence an audience and get your ideas across is crucial for success. Follow these six principles for communicating powerfully.

   o Seize the audience's attention by starting your narrative with a compelling story, video, quote, question or data.

   o Leverage the power of three by presenting three ideas, three points or three steps, rather than eight or nine; as content grouped in threes not only sounds more pleasant, it is also easier to remember and comprehend.

   o Add weight to your statements by quoting credible sources.

   o Strengthen your narrative by incorporating stories as well as facts, thus appealing to both the right and the left brain.

   o Engage the audience by using visually descriptive language incorporating metaphors and similes.

o Use the right language when engaging in a sensitive context such as performance management or conflict resolution. Follow the below principles:

- Separate facts from interpretation

- Be specific while stating facts

- Use tentative language to state your interpretation

- Use the 'I' rather than 'you' language as the latter, by sounding accusatory, tends to put the other person on the defensive

References

1. Goyal M. How India's workforce participation rate of women has sharply declined over the years. The Economic Times [Internet]. 7 March 2020. Available from: https://economictimes.indiatimes.com/news/company/corporate-trends/how-indias-workforce-participation-rate-of-women-has-sharply-declined-over-the-years/articleshow/74531505.cms?utm_source=contentofinterest&utm_medium=text&utm_campaign=cppst

2. Land G. The failure of success. TED Talk [Internet]. Available from: https://www.youtube.com/watch?v=ZfKMq-rYtnc

3. Hill LA. Becoming a manager: how new managers master the challenges of leadership. Brighton: Harvard Business School Press; 2003.

4. Harvard Business Review [Internet]. Frontline managers: are they given the leadership tools to succeed? Available from: https://hbr.org/sponsored/2016/04/frontline-managers-are-they-given-the-leadership-tools-to-succeed

5. Sandberg S. Why we have too few women leaders. TED Talk [Internet]. Available from: https://www.ted.com/talks/sheryl_sandberg_why_we_have_too_few_women_leaders?language=en

Your Action Plan

You had carried out a personal brand audit comprising the following steps in chapter 1.

1. Introspect on the key elements of your brand.

2. Understand how your stakeholders perceive you.

3. Identify gaps between your self-perception and the way you are perceived by others.

4. Design a plan to bridge gaps, if any.

5. Identify elements that you need to add to your brand in the context of your goals and your next career move.

Now revisit these steps and prepare a robust action plan for enhancing your brand based on the various opportunities for introspection that were provided and the insights that you may have gained from reading the book.

CALL FOR ACTION

1. **Introspection**

   - Identify your top five strengths
   - Identify your top five developmental areas
   - Identify your values
   - Identify your passions and interests
   - What sets you apart from your peers?

2. **Validation**

   - Identify five people with whom you have interacted in different work situations, who know you well and are likely to offer candid feedback. These could be your manager, clients, peers or direct reports.

   - Ask them the following questions and document them in the Table 13.1.

     o How do you perceive me?

     o Name five areas of strength and five areas of improvement that you have noticed.

     o What can I do differently to be more successful?

   - Manage your reactions appropriately and resist the temptation to explain, defend or express disappointment. Ask for examples or clarification, if required.

   - Thank the person sincerely for the feedback.

   - Use the Table 13.1 to record your self-perception and the feedback received from your stakeholders.

Table 13.1.

Parameter	Self	Team	Manager	Client
Strengths				
Developmental Areas				
Values				
Passions				

3. Reflection

- Analyse the data you have captured in Table 13.1 by reflecting on the following questions:

  o What are the common themes that are emerging?

  o Is there any deviation between your self-perception and the way others perceive you?

    i. Are there any strengths that you believe you have, which others have not noticed? *Think about ways to display these strengths such that your stakeholders notice them.*

    ii. Are there any developmental areas that your stakeholders have pointed you to that you were not aware? *How will you act on this feedback?*

4. Adjustment

- What are your goals for the next two years?

- What skills, knowledge and behaviours do you need to inculcate so as to position yourself well for meeting these goals?

- What actions do you need to take in order that your brand manifests these skills, knowledge and behaviours? How will you demonstrate these?

5. **Your Action Plan**

   Design and document your action plan for augmenting your brand along the four dimensions of a personal brand discussed in the book.

Table 13.2.

Dimension	Action Plan
Substance	
Connect	
Visibility	
Wrapping	

ABOUT THE AUTHOR

Charu Sabnavis is an executive coach, facilitator, diversity expert and a columnist.

Disimpassioned with the principles of economics, Charu, an alumnus of Delhi School of Economics, embarked on an enriching and challenging journey in the field of people and organizational development after a successful corporate stint, wherein she spearheaded HR, learning and development and operations at Morgan Stanley, Capgemini, Datamatics and NIIT.

She started Delta Learning, a company specializing in organizational and people development, in 2012, and has trained and coached over 8,000 people in 55 organizations across six industries in the areas of leadership, workplace excellence and diversity. She has engaged with teams at PricewaterhouseCoopers, BNP Paribas, Deutsche Bank, Capgemini, Bank of America, ANZ, HDFC Bank, IDBI Bank, NSE, CRISIL, MCX, NCDEX, Aegon Life, Birla Sunlife Insurance, Future Generali, Larsen & Toubro and Tata Power among others.

She is associated with the academia, teaching business communication at S. P. Jain Institute of Management & Research and National Institute of Securities Markets.

Her tryst with the print media dates back to 2005, when her first article was published in the *Economic Times*. She surged ahead with her writing career publishing articles on workplace effectiveness, diversity and leadership in the *Mint, Financial Express, Business Standard, Hindu Business Line, DNA, Mumbai Mirror* and *Hindustan Times*.

When she is not coaching and training people, Charu enjoys hearing Indian classical and Blues music, tending to plants and practising yoga.

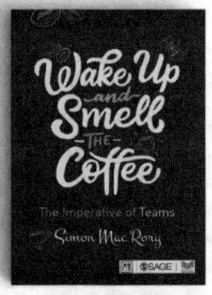